DANGEROUS HOPE

Planting Something Meaningful in the Soil of Disappointment

Mandy B. Anderson

Copyright © 2021 Mandy Anderson, penname Mandy B. Anderson

Published in the United States by RAYMA Team Media, a division of RAYMA Team, LLC. www.raymateam.com

1st Edition

Copyright in Bismarck, North Dakota

All rights reserved.

No portion of this book may be reproduced, stored in a retrieval system, or transmitted in any form or by any means – electronic, mechanical, photocopy, recording, scanning, or any other – except for brief quotations in critical reviews or articles, without the prior written permission of the publisher.

For permissions contact: info@raymateam.com or visit www.mandybanderson.com.

Paperback Print ISBN: 978-1-7366356-4-3

Hardcover Print ISBN: 978-1-7366356-5-0

E-book ISBN: 978-1-7366356-6-7

Cover Design by: Mandy Anderson

Photography by: RachaelNevaPhoto.com

ADVANCED PRAISE FOR DANGEROUS HOPE

•••

"In a story that is personal, practical, and positive, Mandy reminds us that hope is a long game, and gives us tools and encouragement to stay the course and see the good results in our own lives. An encouraging read for anyone facing the setbacks and disappointment that we all encounter at different times of life."
~ **Rachel Linden, author of** *The Enlightenment of Bees*

"*Dangerous Hope* is a heartfelt and inspiring read that will make you laugh, gasp, and cry in equal measure. Mandy B. Anderson has a lighthearted way about her that makes the reader fall in love with her story and desperately root for her to win. The advice and wisdom in the pages of this book are tangible and came at a steep price. Her courage is inspiring."
~ **Meggan Larson, Best Selling Author, Coach, and Course Creator**

"Anderson captured the essence of living with a chronic illness and not allowing said illness to defeat your ability to hope. What is Dangerous Hope and how does one enter into it? Read this book! You will discover it is exactly what you need without realizing you needed it."
~ **Darla Medeck-Johnson, author of** *Dewdrops to Raindrops*

"Mandy captures the delicate dance with hope through living with a chronic, life-threatening illness in such a powerful way. In the midst of struggles, she beckons the reader to rise up and hold onto hope when it doesn't make sense. Her coaching skillset shines radiantly as she walks us through how to cultivate hope in any circumstance."
~**Lara Govendo, Mental Health Counselor, Author, and Speaker**

"There are times when hope is all we have. If you have ever rolled up in a ball in a corner, afraid to hope, but knowing that hope is all that is left, you need to not just read, but truly digest *Dangerous Hope*. Mandy B. speaks her truth, creating a safe place for you to tell your truth. Then she guides you through a real life process of taking action and being mindful."
~**Kim Nagle, author of** *The DAMN Plan: How To Find Freedom, Love And Money In Your Business.*

"This is a must-read for anyone who has struggled with hope and has dreams that are big & scary. This book will reignite your passion for living life to its fullest through The Cycle of Dangerous Hope!"
~ Jen Winterberg, Entrepreneur and RAYMA Team client

"Mandy B. Anderson tells her story while inspiring ours in a way that encourages reflection and a knowing in the worth of our Dangerous Hopes."
~ Valerie Schoepf, Community Health and Wellness Advocate

"This book will empower and challenge those that read it to dig deep within themselves to bring to surface their innermost hope. Thank you, Mandy, for inspiring me to explore hope at an entirely new level."
~ Tara Cherie Hayes-Johnson

"Mandy B. Anderson has led us on an intimate journey through her fields so that we can begin to truly see our own, naked and imperfect as they are, and made attainable their potential by providing focus, definition, and action."
~ Carleen Soule

"Mandy's wisdom is beyond her years. As a 63 year old woman, I read her book and learned so much that many may never come to understand in all our years. Thanks, Mandy, for teaching this old lady a few new tricks."
~Susan Beehler, Small Business Owner and RAYMA Team Client

"This book entered my life at the right time. I found so many tools that I could use not only in my personal life, but professional as well. The raw and open vulnerability that Mandy B. Anderson shares is astounding. We are not alone in the struggles and we can rise above our circumstances as long as we have hope. Excellent read!!!"
~ Sunne Modin, Small Business Owner and Former Client

"5 stars — an unapologetically realistic delivery packed with emotion! I can't imagine how challenging it would be to give a voice to Dangerous Hope, but I do know that Mandy did it with a grace only a talented author like herself possibly could."
~ Sabrina Walker Hernandez, CEO of Supporting World Hope

DEDICATION

•••

To my dad. I cherish our coffee dates and deep conversations more than words could ever express.

BY MANDY B. ANDERSON

•••

In Sickness and In Health

UNASHAMED

She Who Overcomes

UNRUSHED

She Cultivates Resilience

Truth Statement® Journals available at
www.raymateammedia.com

CONTENTS
•••

ONE
The Only Thing Stronger Than Fear 1

TWO
A Crucial Understanding of Hope 23

THREE
Sowing the Seeds of Dangerous Hope 49

FOUR
The Weed of False Hope 71

FIVE
The Mulch of Hope Deferred 103

SIX
The Cycle of Dangerous Hope in Business 135

SEVEN
Becoming an Agent of Dangerous Hope 159

Acknowledgements

Notes

ONE

The Only Thing Stronger Than Fear

Not everything you throw in the toilet sinks to the bottom. It's probably common sense when you think about it. However, back in March 2010, I was a bit stunned when my medicine floated at the top like it was begging me not to flush it. Those little enzyme capsules designed to help me digest my food so I can be at a healthy weight — yeah, they didn't sink after I tossed them in. They just bobbed in the water and floated together like a silent army.

And then I flushed them.

The breathing medication came in plastic ampules and little glass jars. It seemed a bit too risky to flush those down the hotel toilet. I threw those away in the trash can instead. But the enzymes — for some reason flushing those down the toilet seemed like the ultimate line in the sand. It was the most dramatic gesture I could think of to activate my hope of being miraculously healed.

I stood there in the hotel bathroom, in my pajamas and wet hair, and I flushed the medicine that had kept me alive for 28 years. For years I had heard stories of people who had been miraculously healed of diseases that there were no cure for. People who had gone to a prayer service, been prayed over with anointing oil, and suddenly could walk after being paralyzed for months or years, or their cancer suddenly vanished, or even lupus was suddenly gone forever. I so desperately wanted to experience a miracle like that in my body. I could still smell the anointing oil that had been poured over my head during prayer time earlier that evening. Even after washing my hair, the heavenly scent of frankincense lingered for days.

Looking back now, it's hard to tell what I actually flushed down the toilet that night: my hopes or my fears. Maybe it was a little bit of both. All I know is that this action marked my first act of Dangerous Hope. You'll know the full story by the end of this book. I will tell you now though, it didn't go the way I hoped it would. Not even close.

You see, I was born with cystic fibrosis, an incurable genetic disease that affects the respiratory and digestive systems of the body and limits the ability to breathe over time. I have to take breathing treatments two to four times a day to loosen up the abnormally thick mucus in my lungs so I can cough it out and breathe. I also have to take digestive enzymes to help digest the nutrients from food because that thick mucus also resides in my digestive system, blocking my body's natural enzymes from reaching the pancreas. Malnutrition is a major symptom of this disease. All of this takes a toll on patients, like myself, and our families physically, emotionally, mentally, and financially. Until recently, the only hope that we had in the CF community was that if we adhered to our medications, we could delay lung infections that could lead to needing a lung transplant, or even death. Without daily medications, that hope is nonexistent.

Hope. As humans, we hope for so many things. We hope for our circumstances to change. We hope for our businesses to succeed. We hope for equality, for justice, and for positive change. And we hope we can cure disease. Hope is the belief that what you want can be obtained, or that things will turn out for the best.

Stories are powerful. I'm a total nerd who loves books and coffee, and I love fandoms more than any grown woman in her late thirties should! I nerd out on all the fandom theories of the Marvel Comics Universe, *Harry Potter*, and yes, even *Twilight*. But my absolute favorite story is *The Hunger Games* series. In the movie based on the book, the villain — President Snow — says this, "Hope. It is the only thing stronger than fear. A little hope is effective, a lot of hope is dangerous."

I've been thinking about that line for quite some time now, and as much as I hate to admit it, the villain is right. Hope *is* dangerous. As I've chewed on this message for the past few years, I realized hope is dangerous for two reasons:

REASON #1:

Hope is dangerous because if you hope for something and don't get it, you risk disappointment. I have struggled with this, and know this dance all too well. And I know I'm not alone. We all dance this tango of disappointment, not knowing how to tear our eyes away from the sultry chaos in front of us.

Maybe you've been there too, or you're in this spot right now. If so, I must warn you that there's danger in focusing on the disappointments. While it happens to all of us, I have learned that getting stuck in disappointment will only rob you of what could be. My goal is to help you train yourself to see past the disappointment into the possibility.

REASON #2:

Hope is dangerous because if you hope for something and you get it, you can spark change for generations to come. This kind of spark rises up in a person, fueling them to take action and reach their potential, burning down mediocrity and excuses. Hope that blazes like this cannot be snuffed out. It burns bright for all to see! I've tasted these wins in small, hors d'oeuvres sized portions and they've left me wanting more each time.

In my work as a Leadership Coach and Certified Life Coach over the last seven years, I've noticed that people really wrestle with hope when things get hard or take too long. It can be so devastating when we start to feel unsuccessful in the endeavors we are hoping to succeed in. That's when we find ourselves scouring the internet for evidence that hope is indeed still possible. A simple Google search of the words "how to be successful" will provide you with 1,160,000,000 results. The human race is hoping for success and googling how to get it, searching for a guide through the process.

The art of planting is perhaps one of the simplest forms of Dangerous Hope. It can help us grasp the realities of what the process of hope looks and feels like. Farmers hope for a big harvest, but they know that they must participate in the process. Yes, they understand that they can't control all of the variables, but they also understand that the work of their hands is one of the biggest variables to the success of anything they plant.

My father was a farmer. During hot summer days on the North Dakota plains, he would work the fields with my grandfather. No, they didn't plow their fields by oxen or with a pitchfork and a hoe. It was the 1980s, and they used an air-conditioned combine, letting me ride along sometimes.

My little legs would walk through the dusty, scratchy fields and my dad would lift me up to the ladder where I would climb into the equally dusty cab. What I saw out the giant windshield captivated me. I would sit on the floor as close to the glass as I could get and watch the header cut the plants. I was mesmerized by the perfect lines of crops; they satisfied my OCD in a manner that only fellow OCD peeps can understand. Then I would glance back and see the wheat shooting into the grain cart. I could never figure out how they separated the grasshoppers from the wheat. Clearly some of the bugs were chopped up into little pieces and mixed in with the wheat too, right? I mean, they were everywhere, so they had to be.

My dad quit farming when I was in high school, and the days of farming were long forgotten. In fact, reminiscing about it right now is something I haven't done for years. I can smell the hot summer air and the dirt right now if I just close my eyes and hold my coffee cup in a somber moment of nostalgia. I haven't thought about that time in ages. In fact, the last time I thought about it was on a coffee date with my dad a few years ago.

That day, I showed up with my journal and my favorite pens. He looked at me a bit funny when I explained that I wanted to ask him about farming. Actually, I believe what I said was, "God told me to ask you about farming." In fact, I'm certain that's what I said. It's the only thing that would have made my dad give me a funny look.

"Yeah, I'm supposed to ask you about farming. I don't know why; I just think I'm supposed to learn something. So… tell me about farming. How did you get started? What made you quit? What is the process of planting and sowing?"

Over the next two hours I listened to my dad tell me the fascinating tales of planting and sowing. I'm getting emotional right now just thinking about it, because back then I thought this information was only going to be useful for an upcoming event that I was speaking at. Since then, I have seen how this information has drawn people in and helped them apply life-changing principles to their own lives. And right now, at 7:48 am on a crisp December Friday morning with my coffee cup getting cold, I can see that learning this information a few years ago set the stage for a bigger message than my heart could hold back then: the message of Dangerous Hope.

What my dad shared with me that day remains nestled in the pages of my journal — a pink journal with the words "be bold & shine bright" scripted across the front. It is worn now, as I have referred to the lessons my dad shared with me time and time again while preparing for coaching classes and keynotes. And now I get to share those lessons with you.

Now, I don't have a green thumb at all. In fact, I just threw away a houseplant that I couldn't keep alive. However, what I am good at is seeing lessons within stories and connecting them to real life. The lessons my dad taught me about planting and hope are centered around how your thoughts and actions are like seeds being planted. If you hope for success, you need to be aware of which seeds you are planting. The two keys of a successful harvest that he taught me in a tiny coffee shop on a wintery day back in 2018 are crucial to your success from this point on.

The first key of a successful harvest is this: Prepare for success by planting well. "There were many years we seeded in very dry conditions, and I would think to myself, why am I doing this?" My dad told me this with a nostalgic look on his face as I frantically put my pen to paper to catch every word he said. "If you didn't do a good job seeding, you couldn't expect a harvest. When it was time to harvest, that was the priority."

Naturally I wondered what qualified as "good seeding." He informed me that good seeding meant that you would work the ground and get rid of the weeds. It also meant you would have to be precise about seed placement. Depth mattered. So did concentrating the nutrients around the seed so it could grow. He told me that the old school way of giving seeds nutrients was to spread the nutrients across the whole field. Doing this would hopefully get enough nutrients to the right seeds. It worked for thousands of years that way until the modern age found a better way — a more efficient way. Now days, farmers concentrate the nutrients so they fall right on the seeds. This stops them from wasting the nutrients — the resources needed for optimal growth. Today, farmers concentrate these precious resources on the area that is going to generate growth.

My dad took a sip of his coffee and then continued sharing his wisdom. "The conditions didn't always look perfect in the seeding. There were times when it was too dry and it didn't rain. You would be tempted to cut back on your investment. But we always swung for the fence and saw God provide during the harvest. Your job is to seed by faith; God's job is to bring the harvest. But, when harvest time arrives, your job is to work and catch it all while it is there."

Part of preparing for success with a good planting system meant that you would have to map it out. Every year my dad and my grandpa would map out their fields. Then they would plan ahead as to what would go where the next year, and what needed to be changed. They had five different crops. They planted and harvested barley first. Next was wheat. They would plant and harvest this second. Canola and lentils would be third in line on both ends of the process. And finally, sunflowers.

"The farming process works in business, too," my dad said. "In business, your crops are your services and products. You diversify them so you have consistency in revenue. Don't put all of your eggs in one basket. In farming, you never knew which crop had more of a demand in the market that would drive up the price. The same goes in business."

The second key to a successful harvest is to develop a good root system. My dad explained that when things were taking root, you would have to control the weeds. But then as they grew, different types of weeds would grow along with them. There would be fewer weeds, but they would be larger weeds. You needed to control them because they would make harvest horrible if you didn't. My dad told me, "Little weeds keep the crop from even getting started. Weeds that come later on hinder your harvest."

He also mentioned that the health of the root depended on how you prepare the seed beds. You had to till the ground and move the crops around each year.

"You also need to remember that you need mulch," he said.

"Mulch?" I replied.

"Yeah. Mulch. You have to work the straw into the ground. It builds up the organic matter which makes the ground fertile. This holds the moisture in and keeps the sun from drying it out. You must work the mulch into the seedbed to help the seeds grow. The funny thing is that some farmers would burn their crops instead. It was a shortcut to not working the fields — only it backfired on them. They ended up with no organic matter, no mulch, to work into the ground."

Mulch makes the ground fertile and helps generate a bountiful harvest. When it comes to Dangerous Hope, the mulch of life is discouragement and disappointment, setbacks, and hard times. Those are the kinds of organic matter that we are supposed to work into the soil of our lives to keep our hope growing. That's what actually brings success to fruition. And when we take a shortcut and skip working the fields — in this case we skip the processing — we have no organic matter to work into the ground in which we plant our hope.

"Dad, is there ever a time when burning your crops is good?"

"Yes," he answered. "Burning your crops is good when you've lost control. When there is too much organic matter and your slews are running amuck, then burning your fields might be necessary. But you must realize that if you burn it down, you have to rebuild it back up and you will start with nothing. Burning brings more risk of erosion."

In life, some people burn down their fields. They find themselves at a brand-new start. But often, they don't prepare for success or develop a good root system. They end up with erosion in their life and then they just keep falling into the same patterns. And then there are the people that do it differently — with wisdom. They burn their fields and lean into the process of rebuilding with Dangerous Hope. They intentionally start over from scratch by learning from their mistakes and taking the advice of successful people that have gone before them. They go through counseling. They get the accountability they need to be able to handle the strong winds that threaten to bring erosion.

"If you didn't risk caring, you'd have no organic matter in your life. You would wither up and die," my dad said.

I nodded in agreement as I scribbled those words in my journal. I had a strong sense of what it felt like to wither up and die inside, because I had felt that way only two years after flushing my medication down the toilet.

My dad ended the story that day by telling me that he farmed for a total of seventeen years. He was 37 years old when he quit. Three years later we moved to Fargo, North Dakota and that's when my dad moved into the six-figure club financially. His wisdom in financial planning opened the door to him helping my grandpa sell the farm when the time came.

I'm typing this up on December 18, 2020, just after my 39th birthday. Looking at my dad's story of farming and then transitioning into a successful career at the age of 40 gives me hope. It encourages me because right now, I'm in the season of swinging for the fence. I'm working the land of my dreams and I've yet to get a taste of the big harvest I've been dreaming of. I'm sure there is mulch I haven't fully worked into the ground yet. I'm sure there are crops I need to rotate in order to diversify better. What brings me the most hope right now is realizing that, even though statistically I shouldn't be alive right now, I've still got time. I'm not too old. I haven't missed my shot or aged out. A few years ago, I burned down a field and I've just been doing my best to rebuild it. But you know what? It takes time.

If you've had moments in your life when you've burned down your fields in order to take a shortcut, and now you're living in the reality of erosion wondering where it all went wrong, I pray that my story encourages you. It's not too late. You, too, can begin planting the seeds of Dangerous Hope and start fresh. My hope for you is that this book will be the guide that will help you do exactly that.

MY HISTORY WITH HOPE

I know a thing or two about planting the seeds of hope, losing hope, and finding hope again. It's been the recurring theme of my life. I think it's the story I am destined to tell. In fact, I'm only alive today because someone decades ago dared to hope for a cure for the disease that is woven into my DNA. The cure is yet to be found; however, because someone dared to even hope for a cure, the lifespan of my people has been lengthened dramatically and our quality of life improved.

My people. This is the first time I've ever referred to other CF people as "my people" — as though I'm the leader of a band of misfits determined to storm the castle and claim victory over our captivity.

It's not that I've hidden my CF or been coy about it. I'm pretty much an open book if you give me coffee and sit with me one-on-one. I've just never proudly claimed the CF community as my own because I've been too busy fighting the stigma of having a disease. I've always tried to live outside the box of CF — tried to prove that it doesn't own me, doesn't define me, doesn't limit me. Although there is so much more to my life than just the story of cystic fibrosis, something feels right about claiming it and seeing it as an ally instead of an enemy. I'm standing in solidarity and using the gift of my voice to shine a light on this disease and advocate for it. I do this because of it. I'm not so sure we can ever truly hold that which we hope for until we can understand what we have and where we are coming from.

In 1981, the medical outlook for a baby born with cystic fibrosis was not good. It was known as a child's disease because children rarely reached adulthood due to its life-threatening severity and complications.

Sixty-five red roses symbolize this disease, a beautiful symbol for a treacherous illness known for suffocating its young victims to death. That was the reality of cystic fibrosis in 1981. The story goes that a child once had difficulty pronouncing "cystic fibrosis" so she would go around telling people that she had "sixty-five roses" instead.

When my mother was pregnant with me, she visited a friend whose baby girl had recently been diagnosed with cystic fibrosis. My mother observed her friend giving her baby percussion, a therapy used to help loosen the mucus in the lungs. With cupped hands, the young mom was lightly pounding her baby's back, chest, and sides. *Thump, thump, thump. Thump, thump, thump.* The rhythmic sounds echoed throughout the room. My mother watched and thought to herself, "I don't think I could ever do that to my baby." It was a passing thought. Looking back though, it was probably a premonition of what was to come.

I was born in December of 1981, a few weeks early. And I only weighed four pounds, nine ounces. When I was four months old, my maternal grandmother, Grandma Agnes, kissed my forehead and told my mom that it tasted salty. Grandma Agnes knew of a distant family member who had been born with cystic fibrosis several years earlier, and she reminded my mom that one symptom of the disease was salty skin. My parents were hoping for a healthy child, and there was a part of them that believed bad things didn't happen to them, so they brushed it off.

Yet, as time passed, it was evident that something was not right with me. At six months old, I weighed only ten pounds and had been diagnosed with a failure to thrive. I was sick with pneumonia or bronchitis often and spent more time in the hospital than a newborn baby should. On Memorial Day 1982, after a long six months of battling this unknown sickness that never seemed to go away, my parents ditched their plans to visit their family and finally met with a specialist who confirmed what they didn't want to hear. I had cystic fibrosis.

In that moment, all their hopes and dreams came crashing down. Life became a whirlwind of learning how to give me breathing treatments twice a day and mixing medication for each one. Doctor visits would now be a monthly requirement. So would pounding my chest so the mucus could be loosened up and I could cough it out. Suddenly the thing my mom thought she could never do became her new normal.

New normal. I'm writing this book eight months into the worldwide pandemic known as Covid-19. The words "new normal" have been thrown around this year left and right as the human race has been shaken by an invisible virus that can cause deadly respiratory symptoms that leave its victims suffocating to death. An invisible virus that suddenly makes us aware of the need to stay home when sick, wash our hands more, cover our coughs, work from home, limit large crowds, and wear masks in public so that we don't risk spreading this virus, which might kill those who are most vulnerable to it. In many ways, it's like the entire world woke up to living with cystic fibrosis in March 2020. That's the reality of life with CF for many of my people. That's what we have had to do for decades in order to stay healthy because a slight cold could turn deadly. And while I have not lived my life in fear, I have known nothing but this life. This world of cystic fibrosis and breathing treatments and doctor appointments and social distancing from my CF friends or others when they are sick.

Growing up, I had a lot of hope. Even though the outlook for CF patients was not great, it was better than it used to be. My parents didn't keep me in a bubble. They taught me to be responsible and that I could do anything I put my mind to as long as I took care of my health. It was that perspective that helped shape me into the woman I am today. The daily responsibilities of life with CF were as basic and boring to me as brushing my teeth; it wasn't something I dwelled on or even talked about; it was just something I had to do each day to stay healthy. I didn't know anything different, so to me, this was just part of living. And I was a very healthy CF patient for most of my life. In fact, I was the model patient and never rebelled. Never skipped a doctor appointment or denied that I had cystic fibrosis. I took every treatment, every pill, every sinus surgery, every hospital stay like a champion.

My parents also taught me about God and my Savior, Jesus. I grew up in the world of church. I was a Sparky in AWANA and I even went to Nationals a few times for Fine Arts. If you know the church world at all, then you know from that last sentence that I was in both a Baptist Church and an Assemblies of God church. My mom's side of the family was Catholic and my dad's side was Lutheran. So really, I've sat in all the pews and experienced many theologies. But for me, it didn't matter what brand of church it was. Church was where I grew close to my Creator and it was where I most used the talent he gave me — singing.

Being a singer was the main thing I had growing up. It's the only thing I wanted to be, actually. Well, that and a writer, but back then I was afraid of writing and sharing my thoughts. So, I sang other people's songs instead. Give me any Celine Dion song and I will work at it until I can sing it as well as she can. I don't say that to brag; I say it to point out that this is a skill I have. A skill that should have been impossible because I have a lung disease that limits my breathing. I worked hard at singing. Since I was an only child, I spent a lot of time alone after school and during the summers when my parents were working. And I spent that time singing. I gave concerts for my stuffed animals and invisible friends, and these concerts helped me improve my singing. I hoped to one day be a singer just like Celine Dion. I didn't have a backup plan.

After high school, I spent one semester in college. I hated it. College was not for me. It was my first experience of CF being a problem for other people. My college roommate claimed that my breathing treatments made her feel sick, and that influenced me to skip my treatments more often. By the end of my first semester, I was put on a 28-day course of at-home antibiotics because I was battling a lung infection that would land me in the hospital if I didn't get on top of it. I moved back into my parents' house, quit college, and worked as a salesperson in a clothing store to save money to put toward recording my own album. I found musicians in my college youth group and got to work writing my first CD called, *This Journey*. (It's finally available on iTunes — 20 years later!)

During this time of my life is when I met my husband, Nate. I'll never forget the first time I saw him. I was singing a solo at Chi Alpha — the college youth group where I found the musicians that helped me record my album. Nate was this tall, dark, and handsome guy sitting in the audience. It struck me as odd that I thought he was so handsome when I had a crush on someone else and usually went for the blond-haired, blue-eyed guys. We eventually met and became friends — best friends, actually. The best thing about Nate is that CF didn't scare him. He was genuinely interested in what my life was like with CF, but he didn't treat me like a sick person who would break.

Nate lived in an apartment that was located inside the biggest Assemblies of God church in the city. He lived there rent-free and in return his job was to lock up the church each night. Basically, he and his roommate were live-in security guards. I would go with him during lockups and we would chat and laugh. It was like he lived in a giant mansion. One evening during lockups, he told me, "My idea of the perfect girlfriend right now is someone that lives in another city so I don't have to see her all the time." I remember replying sarcastically with something like, "Wow! Whoever ends up with you will be a lucky gal!" What in the world?! It makes me laugh out loud now that I think about it. That's the man I married! We were so oblivious to the love story that was happening right in front of us!

We got married in 2002. He was 22, and I was 20. Looking back, I am positive that the threat of a short lifespan because of cystic fibrosis is partly why I was in such a rush to tie the knot. I wanted to experience everything life had to offer.

Married life didn't go as I had hoped and dreamed it would, though. I wasn't prepared for the sudden hardships we would experience right after the honeymoon.

During our first month of marriage, Nate was let go from his job. He eventually found a job working as a manager at Lowe's. I was working as a music secretary at the church he used to live at, and booking concerts to market my album whenever I could. We barely spent time together. Our lives were our work. Working opposite shifts from each other, we fell into a pattern of loving each other from afar and not really spending quality time together. Any free time we had on the weekends was wrapped up in being at church — with me singing and him running the sound booth.

Eventually I gave up on my dream of being a singer. It was just too hard and seemed too impossible. I didn't exactly like giving concerts, either. Back then I was afraid of public speaking and had a fear of forgetting the words to songs while I was singing them. The whole thing gave me anxiety. (I didn't realize back then that anxiety is common among CF patients.) So, I quit. I fell into a life of job-hopping because bills had to be paid; but every two years I would realize how unfulfilled I was and unchallenged I was. I would skip around to a different job trying to fill the void of purpose in my life. In doing so, I gained experience in many different industries. After I left the music secretary position in the church, I spent two years as a bridal consultant in a wedding dress shop. Then I spent two years as a property manager with townhome rentals. Then I went back to the wedding industry through my new dream job as a wedding planner. (Thank you, J.Lo for that inspirational movie!) I spent two years as the Event Specialist in a large hotel. Then I took time off to pursue working on my own as a marketing consultant/graphic designer. This is where our finances took a plunge.

For a full year I tried to make a full-time income working on my own and only contributed to putting us into six-figures worth of debt. I had no clue how to manage my time as an entrepreneur, and networking effectively eluded me. Eventually, I went back to the hotel industry as a **PR Director** in an extended-stay hotel because we needed to get out of debt.

I worked full time at the hotel, and once a month Nate and I would fly across the country to different cities to participate in personal and professional growth seminars. Because we were in so much debt, we had sold our house and moved into an apartment — an apartment that burned down in October 2010. We lost everything. Nine months later, we ended up moving to a different city so that my husband could work in the oil field. That's how we paid off our six-figures worth of debt. We now live in the same community, and I own a company with my childhood best friend, Raychel, who I met at a Baptist Bible Camp in junior high.

That's my story in a nutshell. As you can see from this brief overview, my life has been filled with many moments of things not going as I had hoped. My hopes haven't all been wrapped up in just one thing. It's been a tapestry of hoping for freedom from a disease, hoping for a happy marriage, hoping to get out of debt, and really, just hoping to find my life's purpose.

Hoping for something better has been one of the most dangerous actions I've ever taken. It was dangerous to the mundane reality I fell into. And, it has been dangerous to my future in the best way possible.

You may have noticed that the ups and downs of losing hope and having hope are a thread that weaves throughout my story. The principles of planting hope that I shared in this chapter are just the beginning of turning your disappointments into something meaningful. They are the foundational skills of what you need to know, and I'll be sharing my story of what happened after I flushed my medicine down the toilet to build upon them throughout the rest of this book.

When people lose hope, they become fearful. And since hope really is the only thing stronger than fear, it's time to dive into some crucial characteristics of hope so we understand the process better. We need to be filled with a Dangerous Hope that is so strong it can change our current reality for the better.

We need to be filled with a Dangerous Hope that is so strong it can change our current reality for the better.

TWO

A Crucial Understanding of Hope

Something happens to the human spirit when we get knocked down again and again in life but refuse to stay down. Tenacity, resilience, and courage all grow inside of us. These characteristics are rarely developed any other way. We develop these traits when we refuse to let go of our hope, and when the journey gets hard, we make it matter. Those of us who dare to hope know that this is the secret to not losing sight of what we hope for. We must make it matter.

I learned the importance of making it matter when I found myself in what felt like a hopeless place of depression. I'll never forget what it felt like to look in the mirror and not recognize the face staring back at me.

Two years after flushing my medication down the toilet, I found myself alone in a hospital room struggling to make sense of it all. I slowly pulled my frail 92-pound self out of bed and hobbled over to the bathroom sink, the oxygen tube snaking along with me. I don't recall if I had meant to brush my teeth or my tangled hair. All I remember is the shock of the ghostly face staring back at me. I was in a desperate, dark place.

The face staring back at me with sad, fear-filled eyes was the worst version of myself — the sickest version of myself. My biggest fears were in that face. It was the face of someone dying from cystic fibrosis. I had seen it a few times in my friends with CF who had passed away. I wasn't sure if I could come back from that face. And the saddest fact was that I did it all to myself.

So, I did the only thing left to do.

I made a choice.

And I gave myself a pep talk.

With fierce determination, and the voice of the coach I would one day become, I said out loud, "Mandy, this is not how your story ends. No matter what your new normal is — whether that means wearing oxygen for the rest of your life, or having to take insulin shots for CF-related diabetes, or needing a feeding tube, or all of the above — no matter what, you will make this matter."

Years later, one of my doctors would tell me that my determination to not give up is probably partly why I am still here on the earth. I think she was right.

Part of the process of discovering hope is being willing to accept that bad things might happen along the way. Things we didn't anticipate. Consequences we put into motion from bad choices or mistakes. Troubles we wouldn't have written into our stories, because we all want the happy ending Disney promised.

But guess what? Life doesn't get resolved within the course of ninety minutes. Even after the "happily ever after" scene where you ride off on your horse into the sunset, life continues. Hope is a long game. Read that last sentence again because it is the first thing you must understand and accept about hope. In fact, these are the five crucial characteristics that you need to understand and accept about hope:

1. Hope is a long game.
2. Hope seems easy, but it's not.
3. Hope asks hard questions.
4. Hope rebuilds again and again.
5. Hope challenges our perspectives.

Before I dive into the nitty-gritty details of my story of Dangerous Hope and flushing my medication, let's go a little more in depth on these characteristics.

HOPE IS A LONG GAME

Everything worth hoping for takes time to develop. Just like a field doesn't grow overnight, the things we hope for don't suddenly appear within 24 hours either. I'm always fascinated by stories of people that took a leap of faith to start a business or go after their dream of singing or writing. I love learning how long it took them to get from dreaming about something to living in the reality of it.

For instance, I've heard it said that it took J. K. Rowling seven years to get the first *Harry Potter* book published. She started writing it in 1990 and spent the next five years working on the whole series. Rumor has it she was turned down by 12 publishers before finding the one that believed in her enough to take a chance on it. Her dream of one book has since expanded into seven books, eight movies, theme parks, products, and many other spinoff books and movies. Did she hope for all of that when she first started writing about this magical world? Probably not. But she believed in her story enough to stay in it for the long haul. And now she's a billionaire.

Let's look at a few other inspiring, famous examples:

- Walt Disney for sure understood that hope is a long game. He experienced rejection and failure 300 times before succeeding.
- Thomas Edison kept his hope alive long enough to attempt inventing the light bulb over 10,000 times before he got it right.

- Oprah Winfrey was in her early twenties when she was fired from her job as a news reporter. A decade later she had her own syndicated show and the rest is history.

Each person in these real-life examples held on to their visions long enough to taste victory. And our world is better for it!

What about you? Are you ready to stay committed to your vision even if it takes seven years, ten years, or decades to accomplish it? What if the thing you are hoping for takes a lifetime to reach? Will it still be worth it? If the answer is no, then it's time to question your dedication or your hope. Hope is a long game that will have many highs and lows. You've got to stay the course and be dedicated enough to see the vision through to completion.

HOPE SEEMS EASY

When we first think about hope, it seems so easy. We often fail to realize that hope comes with setbacks. I learned this the hard way. I once believed that nothing horrible would ever happen to me because of the fact that I was born with cystic fibrosis, and well, that was a pretty challenging obstacle to overcome already!

Boy, was I wrong.

On October 12, 2010, I woke up in a hotel room with nothing but the clothes on my back. Our apartment had burned down the night before, and I was devastated. It was only eight months after I flushed my medication down the toilet. While I had been experiencing some setbacks to that decision, such as weight loss and some coughing attacks, I had also been experiencing some amazing results, too. I was running often, and it didn't hurt. That was something I couldn't do prior to the prayer service that resulted in my decision to flush my medication. I figured the setback symptoms were just my body getting used to this new life of being suddenly healed of cystic fibrosis. That's what I kept telling myself, anyway.

I honestly thought I was experiencing an exciting new season of life now filled with an easy hope. I finally went after my dreams of writing and being a speaker. Then the fire happened, and it changed everything. That exciting season got hard. Fast. It was also one of the gloomiest seasons of life I had ever gone through.

Nine months after the fire, we moved to a new city 196 miles away. The apartment we lived in for the next five years faced north. It had buttercup yellow walls. I hated the color of those walls, but I enjoyed the layout of our new home. Even though it felt like a cave that barely got any sun, it was a new start and I welcomed it. The master bedroom had a window that faced north toward the courtyard and a side patio door with a window that faced east. It was here that I learned to embrace the sunshine when it came.

From May to the middle of June each year, the sun would shine perfectly through the patio window for about one hour a day. On those sunny days, I would jump out of bed and open the shades so our fur-baby, Ajah B., could lie on the sunshine spot on the floor and I could enjoy it with coffee in bed.

During the rest of the year, the sun didn't shine quite the same way.

Now, exactly a decade later, in a condo on a canal that leads to the Missouri River, the sun shines all the time in our home because we face southeast. I still jump out of bed to savor it. Although, these days Ajah B. joins me in spirit with fond memories and there is an empty space in the sunshine spot on the floor.

One morning, while savoring my coffee and enjoying the glorious sunshine, I had a thought: It's funny how when the light shines on you, hope seems so easy. It seems… possible.

And when it gets cloudy, gray, and even dark, hope gets hard. In those times, hope can be lost.

I think this is where faith comes in. Not necessarily faith in God, but rather faith that when we are in the darkness of the valley, surely there will come a day again where the sun shines on the mountaintops. We must remember to have faith that just because we can't always see the light shining on us, it doesn't mean hope is lost.

The sun will shine again. Even if it's only for 45 days out of the year in your favorite room while you're waiting for the upgrade to your dream home.

Such is the journey of hope. Even when it gets dark, we've got to learn to have a little faith and trust that the sun will shine again. And in the meantime, find ways to keep hope alive. Get yourself in areas where the sun does shine so you remember the feeling. Remember that the setbacks and disappointments are part of the journey, and they hold necessary lessons of strength, preparing us for the things we are hoping for. Hope seems easy, but it's not. And when it gets hard, we lose hope because we weren't expecting the difficulty.

But sometimes losing hope actually serves a purpose.

HOPE ASKS HARD QUESTIONS

"So, you're saying sometimes it's okay to lose hope?"

Maybe you're asking that question right now. I was asked the same question recently. The woman who asked looked at me with pleading eyes from across the grass. We were sitting in a giant, socially distanced circle in the park. A pandemic doesn't erase the need for connection, and this cancer group was yearning for it. Ten people listened to me share this message that day, and now they were ready to have their questions answered. Here's a secret they don't tell you about hope: Hope asks hard questions.

Sometimes the hardest question to ask, when it comes to hope, is that one. Is it okay to lose hope sometimes?

We don't want to ask it because we fear the answer might be no. I'm here to tell you that if hope truly is a long game, then absolutely there will be times where you lose hope. And it is okay if you find yourself in a state of lost hope right now. It is okay if you find yourself losing hope a few days, months, or even years from now. It's also okay to ask the hard questions. That is part of the process.

When hope feels lost, I take all of my hopeless feelings to the one place that I know will help me make sense of it all: my journal. As I sit myself in my treatment chair, breathing in my medicine and my body gets rocked by the vibrations of my vest, I can process my feelings on paper. These are a few of the hard questions I have learned to ask myself:

- Why do I feel hopeless right now?
- Given the circumstances, was my expectation of what I was hoping for realistic, or unrealistic?
- What proof exists to show me that what I'm hoping for is still possible, just maybe on a different timeline or accomplished in a different way?

My friend, sometimes the worst thing that happens to us becomes the very thing we need to find meaning and purpose. If I hadn't flushed my medication and fought for my life in the hospital two years later, I wouldn't have found a fierce determination to make my life matter. I wouldn't have this message burning in my heart to share with you in this book.

Don't be afraid to wrestle with hope. And when the setbacks happen, disrupt them by asking the hard questions that will lead to solutions. Those hard questions will also lead to helping you find hope again so you can begin rebuilding when life knocks you down.

HOPE REBUILDS

I admire people that get back up after life knocks them down. The ones that take action. Those who never give up on the dreams inside their hearts, no matter how many obstacles they face along the way. Their stories encourage me to keep hoping. I seek them out when I get knocked down. I want to know what they know and learn from their experiences. One thing I've noticed from so many of those individuals is this: They rebuild. Hope rebuilds.

One such person is my friend and personal trainer, April Lund. April is a passionate coach who turned her life around. She went from being an alcoholic to being a coach on a mission to help others get healthier. A few years ago, she had a dream to run in the Olympics. I sat down with her in our podcast studio one day to interview her. She shares her journey, and her passion, in a heartfelt episode entitled, "Your Goals Don't Give a Crap About How You Feel."

At the time of the podcast interview, she was still training for this goal. A few months later, though, things took a turn. On her journey to reach this big, audacious goal, she experienced unexpected health problems. Health problems that caused her to miss the qualifying time she needed to be an Olympic runner. It was a devastating let down for her, but she didn't quit. She maintains an Elite Athlete status and keeps running and pushing herself to rise above the health challenges she faces. Her fortitude is an inspiration to her entire community of clients and friends every day.

Another woman I admire for rebuilding her life and hope again is my friend and fellow coaching colleague, Kim Nagle. Kim has over three decades of experience as an entrepreneur. In a podcast interview, she told me about her rock bottom season that began when she experienced the death of her six-month-old daughter. She found herself with a half million dollars in medical bills that she couldn't pay. Her business was going under and her heart was breaking. Eventually she got back up again. Why? Because hope rebuilds. And Kim had hope.

These women, and women and men like them, inspire me. Their stories remind me that even when those bad things happen, it is possible to rebuild. It is possible to create a better future, even if you carry unimaginable grief in your heart forever. We need to hear stories like theirs so we can be strengthened when hope seems lost. Their stories help us challenge our own perspectives, and that's a good thing.

HOPE CHALLENGES OUR PERSPECTIVES

One of the most basic truths in life is that we get what we focus on. If you focus on fear, worry, and doubt, you'll feel more fear, worry, and doubt. If you focus on possibilities, gratitude, and hope, you'll be able to see more possibilities, you'll feel more thankful, and you'll have more hope. However, this doesn't mean we treat hope like a magical thing. Hope demands that we hold faith and fact at the same time so we can make better decisions moving forward. If hope is a belief and a feeling, then our perspective plays a big role in whether we keep believing in what we hope for. In the moments when the facts look hopeless, we need to embrace the art of challenging our perspectives. How I view my life with cystic fibrosis is a great example of what I mean by this.

- By the time I was 26 years old, I had consumed 250,000 pills.
- I had spent 14,235 hours doing breathing treatments.
- My medical bills added up to $663,000. And most of that was just for daily medications.

These numbers are quite conservative because many cystic fibrosis patients could double or even quadruple some of those numbers for the same number of years. It would be easy to dwell on the problems, don't you think? But that would be a waste of time and a waste of my life, really.

So, I learned over a decade ago to shift my perspective. In order to see the gift in these obstacles and not lose hope, I needed to look for the good and focus on that. Here's how I choose to look at those facts of life with cystic fibrosis:

- 250,000 pills equaled dedication and discipline to staying healthy.
- 14,235 hours doing breathing treatments gave me daily personal reflection time.

- $663,000 in medical bills… this was a little bit harder to find a new perspective in. The best I could come up with is that I helped pay someone's salary and helped put food on someone's table.

Shifting my perspective to find the positive has become my secret to staying hopeful in some of the most hopeless looking situations. It's not a once and done thing, though. Nothing is when it comes to hope. You don't just decide to stay hopeful and then never again wrestle with the emotions of feeling hopeless. Hope is a belief, one that can be fickle if you're not diligent with it.

Hopelessness was a strong emotion that slithered across the hearts of many people around the world in the year 2020. Holding onto hope that year was hard, and shifting my perspective took some dedication. I didn't always get it right the first time.

At the end of January 2020, I was in the Dallas airport flying home with my husband and my parents from a trip to the Bahamas. We had spent seven days at the beautiful Atlantis resort on the famed Paradise Island. With sun-kissed skin and hungry bellies, we wandered into a TGI Fridays for some food. As I sipped my soda, I noticed that the news channels were lit up with the sad news that basketball legend Kobe Bryant had died in a helicopter accident. It happened while we were in the air somewhere between Miami and Dallas. As commentators and journalists uncovered the details of this breaking story, another story was scrolling across the screen about a strange virus breaking out in China. I thought nothing of it and figured it would be a passing story. Just another virus plaguing a world far, far away from the safety of the world I lived in.

February came and went with the shock and awe that only a Super Bowl halftime performance could bring. The country found itself divided on whether J.Lo exemplified what strength should look like in a woman at the age of 50 or whether her pole dancing was actually a horrible act meant to taint our eyes, tempt our men, and groom our children in negative ways.

And then March 2020 arrived.

Within a week we went from being horrified about J.Lo, to being horrified about Tiger King, to being horrified about toilet paper flying off the shelves because the mysterious virus that had graced the news in January had finally landed on our doorstep.

The coronavirus swept the land of the United States and we were thrown into a whirlwind reality of cancelled events and closed restaurants and shops. Kids came home from school on a Friday and never went back. Kitchen tables now housed computers and school supplies so kids could log into online classrooms. Businesses were forced to work remotely, and the shelves in stores were suddenly bare. It was clear that the people's perspective was focused on prepping for the doomsday apocalypse that invaded us with no warning.

I went into the shutdown with the perspective that this would not be that hard. After all, I've had to social distance from people before. Two-week hospital stays were basically like being quarantined away from people, so this should be a breeze. Move over, fearful people, and let the CF pros show you how it's done!

However, after a solid month of showing up on Zoom calls to motivate people and hosting socially distanced birthday parties in the park so I could be with my best friends but still stay six feet away from them, I started to grow weary. My hope grew fickle and began fizzling out. Nate's work schedule actually picked up during this time because companies needed better technology to meet the demands of this new world we found ourselves in. Since he worked for an audio/tech company, his job was not in jeopardy. But he was gone a lot. And the loneliness of being in an 800 square foot apartment all by myself with no dog, nowhere to go, and nobody calling to check up on me became too much to bear.

There were days in a row where I would wake up and not hear a human voice talking to me until late evening when Nate called me. Mental health advocates were encouraging people to reach out to others for help. I did that, yet it didn't seem to matter. The phone remained silent. I started thinking, "What's the point of asking for help when no one follows through with actually helping?" My counselor at the time even cut my session short, failing to recognize the lifeline he was for me and my need to have someone to talk to. I fired him and looked for a new counselor instead.

I started focusing on the quiet. The loneliness. The lack. It felt as though I really was irrelevant and wouldn't be missed if I just picked up and left it all behind. I was alone. At least if it was my choice, then it wouldn't hurt so much. I could choose to lock others out instead of feeling like I was on the outside looking in. That seemed like the strongest thing to do at that point — put on my armor of a hard heart and stone face.

I wasn't suicidal at all. Not once did I think about killing myself; however, there was one wretched day where the quiet was so loud that I found myself huddled in a ball on the floor, sobbing. My husband called me several times that day to make sure I was okay, and probably to make sure I was alive, to be honest. It was a bad day.

But at some point during the afternoon I sat down with my journal and let all of my feelings out. I wrote angry letters about how I felt so unappreciated and invisible. I let myself get it all on paper so I could do what I knew would help — shift my perspective.

Hope challenges our perspectives.

In the pages of my journal that day, I realized that I was focusing on what I didn't have, when I should have been focusing on what I did have. Here's what it looked like in the category of what I didn't have:

- My best friend wasn't calling me or checking up on me. We worked together, so that made it even harder. I felt like I was irrelevant in both my business and my friendship.
- A friend I reached out to for emotional support didn't even acknowledge my message. I could see that they read it, but there was no response even days later.

- My other friend didn't seem to appreciate the fact that I put together a socially distanced birthday get together for her, and she kept saying that nobody cared about her.
- And my husband wasn't home. He was gone for weeks at a time.

After I wrote down all the ways I felt invisible and the feelings that I had, I started thinking about more than just myself. I started to consider that maybe this was just as hard on everyone else as it was on me. Our circumstances were just different. Here's what my new perspective looked like:

- My best friend isn't trying to ignore me. She was thrust into a world of homeschooling and trying to run a business at the same time. She has five people in her house and they can't go anywhere, so she is just trying to keep it all together and not lose ground on the healing and strength she had experienced from past traumas. This is hard on her, too.
- My friends who aren't replying or don't seem to see how much they mean to me are going through things, too. This is hard for everyone and they need grace, too.
- The feeling that "nobody calls me or cares about me right now" is actually a lie. I have something that many people wish they had right now — a husband that calls

me to tell me he loves me often. Even when I feel ignored by other people, Nate is a solid, steady rock for me to lean on.

Finding this truth in the new, challenging circumstance of the pandemic helped me feel better. It forced me to see things through the eyes of grace. And, it helped me realize the strength I had, because there was a time in my past where this situation could have caused me to be suicidal.

Hope challenges our perspectives. When we take the time to lean into this basic characteristic of hope, it becomes apparent that the story we are telling ourselves might be a fable. If you've experienced circumstances beyond your control and you've lost some hope, then I encourage you to use my stories of challenging my own perspective as a guide to challenge your own perspectives. You just might find that hope has been lost because you've been focusing on the wrong thing.

DANGEROUS HOPE IS A CYCLE

When we accept these five crucial characteristics of hope, it helps us to not feel so hopeless when disappointments come. However, not all hope is created equal. When it comes to planting the seeds of Dangerous Hope, it's not a straight line that goes from Point A to Point B. It's not even a squiggle that winds back and twists and turns.

One of the nerdy qualities that I have, besides loving books and fandoms, is that I get totally stoked about personality tests. Learning about how people think and are wired is a total trip for me! I probably should have stayed in college and gotten a degree in psychology. I've spent the last decade digging into different personality tests, and one thing I've learned about myself is that I am an INFJ on the Myers-Briggs 16 Personalities Test. I have a secret board on Pinterest where I pin INFJ memes and phrases because Pinterest always gets me.

I used to think that my struggle with hope was just part of my personality. It went like this: I got my hopes up and was excited. Then I got knocked down, and it didn't go the way I had planned so I became sad and all doom and gloomy. After a few days of sadness, I got my hopes up again. And eventually I got knocked down. It kept repeating over and over again and I honestly thought that was just the special kind of hell I get to live in as an INFJ.

It's not just an INFJ quality though. What I've learned from listening to the stories and the vulnerable questions of others is that the up and down emotional rollercoaster ride of hope is something that we all experience.

But what if we stopped referring to it as an emotional rollercoaster? What if we quit beating ourselves up, wondering what's wrong with us when we feel discouraged and hopeless? What if, instead, we recognized the emotions for what they actually are — just part of the process? A cycle rich with opportunities designed to help us grow into wise people that can handle the things we are hoping for.

If the journey of Dangerous Hope flows like a cycle that closely parallels the process of planting, it would look like this:

THE CYCLE OF DANGEROUS HOPE

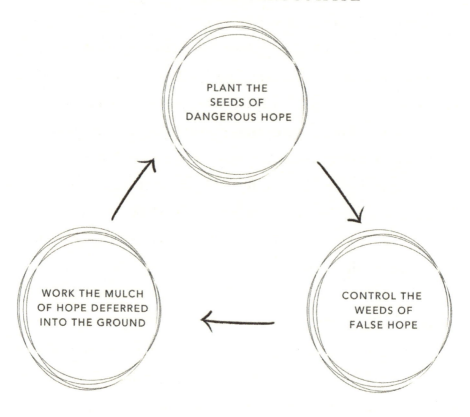

DANGEROUS HOPE

It starts when we plant the seeds of Dangerous Hope. We take a courageous step toward the thing we are hoping for and we begin working our field. We start that business; we raise money for that charity; we sign up for that fitness class; we learn about that cause so we can become an advocate for justice.

There are many seeds that bloom into Dangerous Hope, but some of the main ones that we tend to sprinkle on the ground first are action, boldness, and belief. These are the seeds needed to start. As we grow our field of Dangerous Hope, we add in the seeds of resilience, experience, discernment, and wisdom.

Dangerous Hope is hope that takes action. It builds and rebuilds. It gets back up again and again. It finds the purpose to make things matter. It's dangerous because bad news doesn't stop it, setbacks don't derail it, and not even death can snuff it out because it ends up living on in the lives of those it touches.

When we plant the seeds of Dangerous Hope, we embrace the motto "Make it matter." It's the phrase we remind ourselves of over and over again as we start out on this new journey and it helps us stay focused on the next step.

FALSE HOPE

Every farmer knows that in order to make something matter, you've got to be committed to developing a good root system. This means you've got to control the weeds. Soon after we plant the seeds of Dangerous Hope, the weeds of False Hope pop up. If we don't have good planting processes, we might not even recognize the weeds for what they are.

I hopped on the Google and did a little research on weeds, and what I discovered is fascinating. There are three major classifications of weeds. They are annual weeds, biennial weeds, and perennial weeds. The University of Massachusetts Amherst describes these weeds like this:

> "An annual weed is a plant which germinates, flowers, sets seed, and dies within a single year. All annuals spread only by seed.
>
> Biennial weeds usually live for two years.
>
> A perennial is a plant which lives for many years, and does not die after flowering."

Another source mentioned that "annual weeds grow from seeds from the previous growing season while perennial weeds grow from established roots that survive winters."

False Hope is a perennial weed that massively hinders the harvest of hope and grows from established roots of wishful thinking. It can live on for years and years without you ever knowing that it is there. It hides among other weeds, such as procrastination and toxic positivity.

False Hope pretends. It talks about getting back up and rebuilding but always pushes it into the future, procrastinating. False Hope never actively does anything productive because it is either too busy stewing over offense and bitterness of the past, or waiting for everything to fall out of the sky and just land in its lap, or both.

When the weed of False Hope infests our field, our motto becomes, "I hope it all works out." And then we grab a drink and sit on the couch and wait for things to happen to us, rather than actively working to make things happen.

If we don't learn how to identify and control this weed, we will have a horrible time harvesting the seeds of Dangerous Hope that we planted. We might have some growth, but we will keep repeating the same obstacles over and over again until we cut out the root of the weed of False Hope.

HOPE DEFERRED

In the last chapter we learned that in order to get a good harvest, we need mulch. Hope Deferred is the mulch that we need. Hope Deferred is what happens when we experience disappointments and we start to feel hopeless. It is rich with complicated feelings of worry, fear, doubt, questioning your self-worth at times, and often even anxiety and depression.

This is where people get stuck. They start to believe that good things don't happen to people like them. The motto of Hope Deferred is, "I don't want to get my hopes up. I tried that, and it didn't work out." My friend, if all you did was try, I guarantee you gave up too soon! You've got to be so committed that you are willing to seek out guidance from the brave souls that have gone before you. When those words roll off our tongues, we are standing in the midst of mulch that is begging us to work it into the ground.

My friend, I must tell you that working in the mulch is uncomfortable. It requires you to look in the mirror and admit your own faults and let-downs. It definitely demands that you give yourself permission to get real with yourself and process things that you've tried to bury deep inside. Sometimes that means investing your hard-earned money to work with a counselor or a coach that can ask you the hard questions and help you gain perspective. But whether you decide to work the mulch of Hope Deferred into your ground alone or with some guidance, it's gonna take effort. I promise you it will be worth it, though.

Once we work the mulch of Hope Deferred into the ground, our field becomes fertile again and it is ready for another season of growing Dangerous Hope.

Every time we go through The Cycle of Dangerous Hope, our fields become more fertile and our harvest should be more bountiful. We should have more courage, more wisdom, new skills, new perspectives. Our hope should be so strong that no setback can knock us down.

But instead, because we aren't aware that The Cycle of Dangerous Hope even exists, we get stuck in Hope Deferred. We beat ourselves up and question our abilities and then camp out in a dry and barren field wondering what to do next. We can't seem to find our spark, and so we cannot burn our fields and start again. If you've been in this spot, or you're there right now, then be encouraged because you're not alone. I've been there too.

I'm about to share with you the full story of what happened after I flushed my medicine down the toilet. You'll see exactly what sowing the seeds of Dangerous Hope looked like for me. I'll confess where I lost control of the weeds of False Hope. I won't hold back from fully describing my own season of Hope Deferred. And I'll tell you how I finally worked that mulch of disappointment into my fields again to reap a harvest of Dangerous Hope. By the end of our time together, you'll finally know how to plant something meaningful in the soil of disappointment.

Dangerous Hope is hope that takes action. It builds and rebuilds. It gets back up again and again. It finds the purpose to make things matter.

THREE
•••
Sowing the Seeds of Dangerous Hope

Let's go back to the moment when the pills were bobbing in the toilet water. For a split second, I wondered if what I was doing was crazy. I didn't actually believe that I would die from this decision, but I wondered where it would lead and how long I would last without medication if it didn't work out.

The pills were bobbing in the water, and not just a few pills. ALL the pills. Every single one that I had in my purse or tucked away in my suitcase. Like a drug addict desperate for freedom, I drew a line in the sand and quit cold turkey. I wanted to make my life with cystic fibrosis and the years praying for healing matter. In that moment, I was activating my faith in ways I never had before.

Growing up in the church world, especially the evangelical church world, meant that stories of supernatural healing from the Bible were in my face often. I was immersed in the culture of prayer services and healing services. I know that not everyone reading this will understand or even believe me when I share some of the things I've experienced. And I'm okay with that. Your belief isn't a conditional part of me sharing the lessons I've learned.

The first healing service I remember being at was in seventh grade. I was at a church youth convention with nearly a thousand other kids. The kids from my youth group were sitting up in the church's balcony on the last morning of the convention. The speaker that morning got up on stage and said he wanted to pray for a young lady in the crowd that God had put on his heart to pray for. I don't remember everything he said, but I do remember that as he explained some of the medical issues that this girl had, something strange happened in my body.

It started in my toes. A tingling, warm feeling worked its way up from the tips of my toes until it felt like something flew out of the top of my head. It was weird, but also exhilarating. I was too afraid to go down to the stage in front of so many people, so my youth leader and my friends laid hands on me and prayed for me right there. I didn't feel anything after that. I just went on with my life and stayed as healthy as I could.

But the desire to be fully healed of cystic fibrosis never truly went away.

In my late teens and early twenties, I would find myself in many more healing services like that. Sometimes I found myself at the altar for prayer, not because I wanted to be there, but because someone told me to go up there. Seeking a supernatural healing from Jesus became a goal that I couldn't get away from. And I'm not even sure whose goal it was — mine, or the goal of well-meaning people of faith. All I know is that I wanted to experience the God of the Bible in big ways, and so did the people I was around. So, I would go up for prayer whenever I could. Then a few days or a month later I would go to the doctor for a regular CF checkup and my lung functions would be worse than before they prayed for me. The CF was still there.

Looking back now, I see that every time this happened, I would wrestle with hope.

The night that I was prayed for in March 2010, I realized that every time before that had one thing in common. Not once did I put my faith into action. Instead, I would get done praying and go back home to inhaling my breathing treatments before crawling into bed — life as usual for me. So that night, as the anointing oil was poured over my head and my body felt that familiar sensation of tingling and warmth coursing through my veins, I decided this time would be different.

I made the choice to stop doing my medicine so that I could put my faith into action and walk out the reality of being fully, supernaturally healed of cystic fibrosis, like only the blood of Jesus could do.

That was the start of the most dangerous journey of hope I've ever been on.

I flushed my medication down the toilet, pushed away all thoughts of doubt and worry, and chose to ride the wave of exhilaration and faith. I had met other people who had been supernaturally healed of diseases like cancer and lupus and were now living a life of no more sickness. No more medications. I thought, surely this was the right action step to take.

The next morning, I woke up and went for a run across the bridge. I ran a mile and a half. It was the furthest distance I had ever run without coughing and without tightness in my chest. It felt wonderful. With every step I took, my Dangerous Hope grew stronger.

•••

While researching about the farming process and the guidelines that are set for field and seed inspection, I came across this phrase: Inspection at the time of sowing. It's an important part of the process when farmers certify their seed. This process gives the farmers valuable information about their crops and helps them identify any impurities or diseases that need to be taken care of.

We rarely take the time to inspect what we are sowing in our lives at the moment we sow it.

And we should.

We really should.

Every day we are sowing seeds with our actions and our words. We sow the seeds of hope or we sow the seeds of hopelessness. Sowing the seeds of hope sounds like, "I'm hoping for this thing and I'm actually taking action to make it happen." Sowing the seeds of hopelessness sounds like, "Nothing good ever happens to me. It never works out so why even try?"

I've learned that sowing the seeds of Dangerous Hope actually requires sowing many other seeds, as well. They all have to grow together and they grow best when you are intentional about it; when you inspect your seeds at the time of sowing. However, if you didn't know to inspect your seeds at the time of sowing, I'm here to let you know that now is a great time to start inspecting what you've sown in the past. Start now, and over time, you'll grow in the skill of inspection at the time of sowing.

INSPECTING MY SEEDS

I sowed a lot of seeds while also sowing the seeds of Dangerous Hope during this time. Here's an example of a few of the positive seeds that you will need to plant with the seeds of Dangerous Hope.

THE SEED OF ACTION: You will need to take action toward whatever you are hoping for in life and in business. It won't just magically appear because of positive thinking or manifesting it. Your action might look like actually sitting down to write that book you've always wanted to write. It might be starting the business you've always dreamed of. It might even mean going back to school to get a degree. Your action might be having that tough conversation with a loved one or a friend to start healing the hurt that has been blinding each of you for far too long. Whatever you are hoping for, you must take action. Be intentional with it, sow it wisely, and keep sowing it consistently.

My seed of action was flushing my medicine. Gone were the days of praying for something and waiting for it to happen. Nope. I prayed and then I took action when I flushed my medicine, and I kept taking action every time I decided to go running. I didn't completely give up on taking care of my health or become inactive and lazy, I simply changed my course of action from Western medicine to holistic habits only.

THE SEEDS OF BOLDNESS, COURAGE, AND FAITH: You cannot be timid or cowardly when you hope for something. You must sow the seeds of boldness, courage, and faith. Yes, you will still feel fear at times — but feel the fear and do it, anyway. You will need to be bold enough to refuse giving up, especially when other people judge you. You will need to be ready to face difficulties, and even expect them, so you don't get buried under them when they come.

You will need to have confidence that what you hope for can happen, especially when it doesn't look like it's working or you need to grow in some capacity to handle the next step. And if you don't have faith in God or religion, you'll need to activate faith in yourself and in your abilities to follow through. Faith in your ability to learn new skills. Actually, you'll need to activate this faith even if you have faith in God, too.

Flushing my medication and standing firm in my faith was a bold move, and it took courage to stand strong on that decision, especially when some people around me started questioning it. I kept sowing the seeds of faith by digging deep into my Bible. I read the whole thing from cover to cover during this season, and I did a Google search for Bible verses on faith and healing and scoured three different translations to gain a better understanding of God's Word. Then I posted Bible verses on a marker board in my hallway and spoke them out loud every day. It built my faith and helped me write God's Word on my heart.

THE SEED OF ASSERTIVENESS: Assertiveness gets a bad rap sometimes. I think it's because being passive aggressive has been idolized in the age of social media and funny memes. But Dangerous Hope demands assertiveness. You must make every effort to win and succeed — not in a prideful or egotistical way. Actually, pride and ego can sometimes be associated with assertiveness; however, that assumption is actually wrong. When you look up the synonyms of assertiveness, those words are not on the list. Instead, you'll find words like determination, purposefulness, and willpower. Sowing the seed of assertiveness means your ability to be firm in your purpose will grow. And that's a good thing.

Looking back, I realize that this was the season of my life where I learned how to be an advocate for my own health as an adult. I call that a seed of assertiveness. Prior to this experience, I still had my mom with me at doctor appointments and kept my parents in the loop of helping me make decisions. It was a totally new experience to learn how to be my own advocate and make choices on my own. In doing so I obviously made mistakes, but I also learned how to be an assertive advocate for myself and make decisions by reviewing all the options and making my own choices when it came to my health. That was a good feeling. And a necessary skill.

THE SEED OF RISK-TAKING: Anything you hope for requires some level of risk. You can't avoid it. The seed of risk-taking will need to be intentionally sown in order to grow Dangerous Hope. Yes, that means you probably will experience something hurtful or dangerous to your current reality. That's actually the point. If you were truly happy with your current reality, you wouldn't hope for something better or different.

It's good to get out of our comfort zones and take a risk. And I'm proud of myself for sowing the seeds of risk-taking! However, I will confess that my Dangerous Hope action of throwing away my medication to activate my faith and prove a point was not wise. I see that now. It was too risky. I bet the farm and it almost cost me my life. So now, I have the gift of perspective and I take calculated risks instead of being a loose cannon.

Over the last decade I've paid more attention to what seeds I'm sowing in my life. I've learned to give myself time to think things through and grace to process when I made mistakes. That's the beauty of growing Dangerous Hope — you grow more mature in the process. And, when we take the time to go through the process of inspection at the time of sowing, we make better choices.

The actions we take when we are filled with Dangerous Hope are not always smart. They can be quite reckless at times. And that's okay, I think. (But seriously don't play Russian Roulette with your life like I did.) Sometimes the action we take ends up being a giant mistake. But with those mistakes comes wisdom when we dig deep enough to find the lessons in them.

That's the most important thing to realize. When you make a mistake, you've got to be willing and ready to learn from it. Dangerous Hope learns from mistakes.

Many of the clients that I've worked with over the last several years come to me fearing mistakes. They put unnecessary guilt and shame on themselves because of past mistakes or fear of future ones. What I tell them is that every mistake is a stepping stone toward learning and strength.

That thing you are hoping for won't happen without going through the process of making mistakes, failing, and getting back up again. It doesn't mean there is something inherently wrong with you. It's just the nature of the process.

Remember that truth next time you make a mistake or fall flat on your face. Brush yourself off, get back up, and lean into it until you learn from it. And then take the wisdom you gleaned and keep going.

And seriously, learn from my mistakes here. Don't follow in my footsteps. While I still believe that Jesus can heal any and every disease, I now see that sometimes as humans we try to tell him how to do it. That's not faith. That's playing God. I now see God in medicine and his healing through the strengths and talents of medical professionals as they usher in physical healing. And I'm okay with that. Thriving with medicine is way better than struggling without it to make a point.

Through this experience of growing in my faith and sowing the seeds of Dangerous Hope, I've realized that hope is such a complicated topic. And we try to shrink it down and create rules and regulations around it so it's easier to manage. We grasp on to legalistic views in order to gain some sense of control. But I'm here to tell you that we cannot accomplish Dangerous Hope in legalistic ways. We need to be more flexible than that. Yielding, even.

What we hope for, matters. And that means we must be willing to let the process of achieving it evolve. Hoping for a cure for any disease will uncover new discoveries we didn't expect at first. Hoping for justice and equality will force us to come to terms with assumptions and stereotypes that are uncomfortable. Hoping for any positive change will completely restructure our current reality.

Let's address each of these hopes and how they relate to Dangerous Hope.

HOPING FOR A CURE

Hoping for a cure of any disease is an admirable and ambitious desire. In the cystic fibrosis community that I was born into, it's been a mission for over six decades. Recently I did a Google search on "what diseases have been cured" and "what genetic diseases have been cured."

The answers?

According to Medlineplus.gov, "Many genetic disorders result from gene changes that are present in essentially every cell in the body. As a result, these disorders often affect many body systems, and most cannot be cured. However, approaches may be available to treat or manage some of the associated signs and symptoms."

So, if hoping for a cure hasn't resulted in any cures for genetic diseases yet, why do we keep holding onto that hope?

If most genetic diseases cannot be cured, why bother?

Because hope is the only thing stronger than fear — and a lot of hope is dangerous!

Here's a powerful truth to remember: If nobody hoped to cure disease in the first place, there would be no medical advancements. There would be zero solutions because no one would have taken the initiative to find a cure.

The hope of finding a cure for disease motivates and consumes people differently than the hope of just finding medicine. Both are good; however, the former tends to mean more and ends up finding medicine along the way.

Let's look at it this way: Have you ever trained to run a 5K or a half-marathon?

Over a decade ago, I participated in a few CF Great Strides Walks with my family. The distance each time was 5K, or 3.1 miles for my non-running, non-math friends. It was excruciating. Back then I didn't work out and my endurance was pitiful. I remember one year walking in the rain and barely being able to finish the route.

A few weeks after I flushed my medication down the toilet, I challenged myself to start running consistently. In fact, just fourteen months after flushing my meds, determined to never take medication for CF again, I ran my first 5K. It was exhilarating! On a misty, cloudy May evening, I ran the 5K in the Fargo Marathon and finished it in under 40 minutes, which was a big deal to me back then.

Since then, I've run a few more 5K's and shortened my time down to just over 31 minutes. I've also run a 10K and a half-marathon. After training for a half-marathon, here's what I know to be true: Hoping for a bigger outcome actually pushes you further and makes you stronger than hoping for the little outcomes. Think about this in your own life for a moment. I bet there have been times when you hoped for something you considered big at the time and it pushed you to be stronger. You probably would not have grown at all had you not hoped so big.

What we hope for matters.

On the road to reaching 13.1 miles, you end up running the 5K distance of 3.1 miles often. In fact, that becomes your warm up. The same is true on the road to finding a cure for disease. Along the way, creating new medication becomes the warm up and not just the destination. If the destination was just the medicine, the researchers would quit. Mission accomplished. Clock out of work and go home. The cure for disease is the goal of those with Dangerous Hope. The medication is the warm up.

What we hope for matters.

A group of people dared to hope for a cure for cystic fibrosis back in the 1950s and today we have a medication that helps 90% of the CF community to the point that some people have been taken off of lung transplant lists. No, it's not a cure, but it is so very close. This never would have happened had a group of people not dared to hope in the first place.

Hope is dangerous in the best way possible. It's dangerous to the reality of any disease. If you find yourself hoping for a cure for cancer, lupus, MS, or any other disease that affects you or a loved one, I urge you today to keep your hope alive. It matters more than you know.

HOPING FOR JUSTICE AND EQUALITY

Throughout history there are people that have worked the fields of justice and equality with a fervor that inspired more positive change than we could dare hope for. If there was ever a woman that dove head first into the fields of Dangerous Hope, it was Ruth Bader Ginsburg. At a time when women could get fired for being pregnant, and couldn't even get credit at a bank without a co-sign from their husbands, RBG dared to hope for equality and justice for women in the United States. She put her hope into action daily, and never let the losses stop her.

We can all learn from her attitude and commitment.

The other night we watched the documentary, *RBG*. What struck me through this movie was how she held her composure in the moments where she was misunderstood or flat out mocked. She was always prepared. She was always honorable. And she always had the viewpoint that her job was to teach people something. I'm sure there were moments where she made mistakes or possibly put her foot in her mouth — because she's human and it happens at least once to all of us — however, she positioned herself to be a beacon of hope in our nation, even if she made a mistake.

Have you been wrestling with how to handle the hope of equality and justice that is going on in our culture lately?

If you have been wrestling with how to understand or handle this hope of equality and justice, I want to encourage you with a few final thoughts and life lessons inspired by the life and work of RBG that might make it a bit easier.

First, be willing to listen. Growing up in North Dakota meant that I have been surrounded by mostly white faces my entire life. And since college wasn't my cup of tea, I have been pretty sheltered culturally. So, I started leaning in and listening to people that come from different backgrounds, races, and beliefs. I became willing to lean into uncomfortable topics and conversations. In a recent podcast episode with content creator and fellow cystic fibrosis patient, Bobby Foster, we talked about racism and sexism. He is a fellow Life Coach, and I have admired his social media posts for a few years. Bobby had written a blog post for the Cystic Fibrosis Foundation website about being a black man with cystic fibrosis and it stirred me to want to know more about his life and his experience. I reached out to him on Instagram and he graciously agreed to be interviewed. I couldn't wait to listen and learn from him. Bobby discussed how understanding each other is going to take some work and a willingness to hear someone else's story, even if you don't understand it or believe it to be true. Start there. With a willingness to listen. Truly listen — not to defend, but to understand.

Next, we must be willing to believe that what we hope for matters. What others hope for matters, too. It all matters. Every human being on the face of the planet is hoping for something at this very moment. What is it for you? Recognizing that we all have hopes helps us remember what matters most: People. If what you hope for is different from what I hope for, I want you to know that your hopes still matter. They were put there for a reason. I believe they were put there by your Creator and they are connected to your life's purpose. Believing that what you hope for matters helps you stay committed to the journey of going after it.

That's the last thing to remember: Be ready to stay committed. Remember the wise words of Ruth Bader Ginsburg, "Real change, enduring change, happens one step at a time." The hope of equality and justice happens one step at a time. Every hope happens this way, actually. Stop thinking that if what you hope for doesn't happen quickly, that it's not meant to be. Hope is a long game. Stay persistent, one step at a time.

One of the final quotes that stirred my heart from the *RBG* movie was this one — "I got the idea that I could be someone that made the world better." My friend, hold on to the idea that YOU can be someone that makes the world better. And then, wake up each day ready to live that out, whatever it looks like in your sphere of influence.

ACTIVATING DANGEROUS HOPE

Activating Dangerous Hope happens slowly and all at once. It took me years to get to where I flushed my medication down the toilet in an act of Dangerous Hope. I had to get to the point where I was so fed up with healing services and nothing different happening that the risk seemed worth it. You might be flabbergasted by this reality of my history and playing the game of comparison right now, patting yourself on the back for never doing something so stupid yourself. So let me share a slice of my humble pie with you. You do this, too. It just looks different and feels less risky.

Maybe you've been hoping to lose weight. You keep starting and stopping, "trying" different things to get what you hope for. You keep telling yourself that you need someone to keep you accountable and yet you don't make room in your budget to afford a gym membership or a personal trainer. Or you already have the gym membership and you're treating it like a donation. You haven't followed through long enough to go through the process of getting what you hope for.

Or maybe you keep hoping for things to get better in your marriage, but you won't actually go to counseling. The problems keep piling up and you keep sweeping them under the rug or shoving them into a closet to the point where you are now like Monica on F.R.I.E.N.D.S. with a locked closet that nobody knows about. You keep praying about it. You keep asking for prayer about it. It becomes that thing you keep hoping for but really, you are comfortable in the chaos of the known and the unknown scares you.

These examples don't seem as risky as flushing medicine down the toilet and literally risking your life for something. Yet, they truly are. Your health is never something to play around with. Nor are your relationships. You get this one life. Don't waste the precious time you have on procrastination. Get it done, my friend. If what you hope for doesn't go away, it's because it is connected to your very purpose on this planet. Don't waste that.

I don't say any of this to shame you. I've been there, too. The truth is that until you get fed up with where you're at, you won't sow the seeds of Dangerous Hope at all. You'll stay right where you're at. You'll keep praying for change, sitting on your couch thinking it will just show up in your lap one day as long as you keep praying about it.

If that's where you've been, my friend, you can't sow the seeds of Dangerous Hope yet because your land is infested with weeds!

Sometimes that happens. You find yourself in the thick of the weeds just wishing and hoping like that song from the beginning of that 90's movie, *My Best Friend's Wedding*. Remember that? "Wishing, and hoping, and dreaming, and praying…" I loved that show. Oh, the memories. (And that song is so catchy that it will probably be stuck in your head all day now. Sorry, not sorry.)

Other times you find yourself exactly where you should be in The Cycle of Dangerous Hope. You sparked Dangerous Hope by sowing your seeds intentionally, you're well on your way, and then suddenly you wake up one day and your field of hope is covered in the weeds of False Hope. That's what happened to me. The signs were all around me, really.

•••

A month after flushing my medication down the toilet, the coughing attacks started. It was no surprise to everyone around me. They had been hoping this healing was real, but they were also scared that it wasn't. It was a big surprise to me. I had proved my faith was big enough by doing the one thing you should never do with a life-threatening disease. I prayed for God to heal me, and I stubbornly clung to that hope.

I didn't know back then to control the weeds of False Hope. Instead, False Hope felt like the current of a tsunami. It rushed in and washed away the flames of Dangerous Hope before I even knew what had happened. I went from being warmed by the fire to treading water in an ocean of False Hope before I had a chance to blink. There I was, clinging to the debris floating in the water.

I was like Rose floating on the piece of wood in the ocean after the Titanic sunk.

I was like Taylor Swift clinging to her piano alone in the middle of the ocean in the *Cardigan* music video.

You get the picture…

Really, I was the pills bobbing in the toilet water, begging not to be flushed away into oblivion.

That's the thing about planting the seeds of Dangerous Hope. Sometimes we don't realize that some of the seeds we plant are actually weeds. As you activate Dangerous Hope, and sow the characteristics that will help you maintain what you are hoping for, you must watch for the weeds. And the weed that will threaten to destroy your Dangerous Hope the most is the weed of False Hope.

DANGEROUS HOPE

As you activate Dangerous Hope, and sow the characteristics that will help you maintain what you are hoping for, you must watch for the weeds.

FOUR
The Weed of False Hope

When I was about five years old, my Grandma Sharon had a porcelain doll that she kept locked up behind the glass doors of her china cabinet. She called it her "Mandy-doll." With long dark hair, porcelain skin, and a red velvet dress, it really did look like the photo of me she had where I was wearing a frilly red organza dress for Christmas. I've only held that porcelain doll a few times in my life. It was meant to stay on the shelf only. Looking back now, I realize how often I felt like that porcelain doll. Beloved, but metaphorically kept on a shelf so I wouldn't get sick or break.

I remember a conversation with my dad back in 2006 when he was driving me home from my most recent tune-up. Nate was stuck at home recovering from a back injury while I was in the hospital three hours away, so my dad had driven to the hospital to take me home. This was long before my days of going rogue, back when I was still the model patient. Somewhere on the long stretch of road across the flat, North Dakota plains the conversation got deep. My dad admitted that he had treated me like a toy he loved very much but was too afraid to play with for fear of breaking. I agreed, and admitted that yes, I had indeed felt very much like that beloved toy. Stuck on the shelf. Admired. But left out.

Perhaps that is one of the reasons why my imagination was so vivid as an only child. I spent my free time dreaming and pretending I was someone else. Someone else who never had cystic fibrosis.

In first grade I would play in my front yard with a blanket on my head, telling anyone that came by, "I'm Maid Marion!" She was my favorite character at the time, and I took every opportunity I had to place myself in her shoes. Legend has it I even told my first-grade teacher, Miss Monk, to call me Maid Marion and put up quite a fuss when she didn't.

As an only child, I had invisible friends. Well, just one. She was my twin sister and her name was Melissa. I actually convinced an annoying boy in the fourth grade that Melissa was real. My family was at a hotel for my dad's company Christmas party. This boy was picking on my friends and me in the pool. Fed up, I decided to play a joke on him. I told him that my sister Melissa was going to punch him if he didn't leave us alone. He didn't believe me at first, so I went to get her. I got out of the pool and dried myself off. Then I put on the sweatpants tracksuit outfit I had worn over my swimsuit. It had a reversible jacket, but he didn't know that. I left the pool area and then went around the corner and turned the jacket inside out while also pulling my hair up into a ponytail. I also hid my glasses in my pocket. When I walked back into the pool, I wasn't Mandy; I was Melissa. My friends even went along with the joke. I acted all mean and told the boy that my sister said he was picking on them. At first, he was skeptical, but the more that my friends went along with it, the more he questioned himself. It was hilarious! I'm pretty sure I eventually came clean, and we all laughed about it, although I don't actually remember how it all panned out.

Here's the thing about my invisible twin sister, Melissa — she did not have CF. She became an alter ego of sorts. Although, her not having CF made no sense genetically, but I digress.

The point is that I wanted to be myself — without cystic fibrosis.

Mandy. Not "CF Mandy." Just Mandy.

Clearly the world I painted for myself to escape to was one where False Hope ruled. Anything I wanted to be; I could be. Even if that was someone who suddenly did not have the genetic disease she was born with. In False Hope Mandy World, CF didn't exist. It was magically cured and wasn't even a factor.

I've been thinking about these memories from my childhood for a few weeks now, trying to put words to my experience of False Hope. A few nights ago, I had dinner with my parents to celebrate my mom's birthday. We ventured into a conversation about why I went off my medication in the first place.

"I look back now and it seems like you were always trying to be free of this disease," my dad began. "And now, I see a confidence in you to be yourself with this disease that was not there before."

I pondered his words for a moment while I sipped my wine. "I'm not so sure that I was consciously trying to be free of CF. I think I just wanted to experience God in a big way," I explained. Across the table, my mom nodded in agreement. "But also, there was so much pressure from people at church to go up and be prayed for and healed at every chance. It made me feel like it wasn't okay to just be a healthy CF patient. So many people wanted me to be healed of CF and I couldn't get away from it. You guys didn't do that — but so many other people did — extended family members and friends."

"I know!" my mom piped in. "That always bothered me when people would do that to you."

"When you were growing up, your mom and I never prayed for you to be healed of cystic fibrosis, Mandy," dad said. "We prayed for you to have a long and healthy life."

And I've had that.

Once upon a time people like me didn't get a 39th birthday. I'm so thankful that I did, and that I'm not only alive but I'm thriving. And it would be easy to skip over the rest of the story and just lead you astray by sprinkling False Hope around you, too. I could be one of those voices who dismisses your feelings and pumps you up with motivational phrases that sound good but often leave no room for the depth of understanding that only comes through leaning into the discomfort of conflicting emotions and unanswered questions. But that's not what this book is about. False Hope is a real thing that we must confront in order to fully live out the Dangerous Hope that we are yearning for. If we are ever going to turn our disappointments into something meaningful that impacts the world around us, we must be well aware of the patterns we fall into that keep us stuck.

•••

One month after I flushed my medication down the toilet, I found myself at a routine doctor appointment. It was like visiting extended family — family that I saw every month for as long as I could remember. Every month I had a CF Day appointment when I would go to the clinic and check my lung functions, catch up and laugh with the respiratory therapists, and have a chat with my doctor. Being the model patient that I was, it was typically a fun day of socializing for me, with a few inconvenient medical tests thrown in.

I went into this appointment with the expectation that I would see the proof of my miraculous healing on paper. To me, that meant my lung functions would be at 100% or higher. With no treatments.

The proof did not come as I expected it would.

I stood there, breathing in and out slowly until the respiratory therapist told me to take a deep breath. Then, I jumped and squeezed every breath out of me that I could. I should probably mention that the jumping part of this equation is abnormal.

According to my CF Team, I'm the only patient they've ever had that takes an actual physical giant leap into this part of the breathing treatment. Most people stand perfectly still, or at least stand straight. Not me. I put my whole heart and soul into it! It's something I've always done, and I can't even help it. Maybe it's my version of a sports competition, who knows.

So, I jumped. And I blew all the air out of my lungs. And when it felt like I was going to die from a lack of air, I tap danced my feet into the floor with the fervor of a determined warrior dancing at a bonfire the night before an epic battle. Then, upon the direction of my respiratory therapist, I took a deep breath in and finished the test.

The computer screen showed a cartoon of a brick house being slowly blown down. Normally I could blow all of it down. This time, I only got two thirds of it down. I waited anxiously for the number to show up on the screen, trying to hold back tears of disappointment. I already knew, based on the brick house, that this test result wasn't what I had been hoping for. Still, I was quite shocked at what I saw.

75%.

Not 85% like last time. And certainly not 100% like I had been hoping and believing for. Nope. 75% was all I got. I kept trying and did the next two breathing tests, just like I always did. Only this time, the numbers never got better. They just stayed there at 75%.

This is where I must give you some context. Normally, this drop in numbers would warrant a two-week hospital stay where I would be on IVs 24/7 full of strong medications and four breathing treatments a day to kill off whatever bacterium was stuck in my lungs, causing the lower lung functions. The CF world calls this type of hospital stay a tune-up.

That was my history. I was used to my doctor putting me in the hospital when my numbers dropped from 98% to 92%. Surely that was where I was headed, unless I persuaded them otherwise.

I sat down with my doctor that day and did something I don't normally do. I lied. As he went over my medication and asked me what had changed, I acted as though my life was going on as normal. I felt awful for lying, but I had to protect my choices. I reassured him that I felt good, had a lot of energy, and had even started running. Which was all true — I just wasn't doing my breathing treatments. Because I didn't even have the medication anymore.

And I'm not sure how it happened, but he let me leave that day without admitting me into the hospital for a tune-up. Maybe that was the only proof I needed. Surely if my doctor wasn't concerned enough to put me in the hospital, and he just thought that this was part of "aging with CF" and moving from my late twenties into my next decade of life with a disease, then everything was fine! Maybe my body had to get worse before it got better. Maybe that was part of the healing process.

When I left the clinic that day, I had no clue that my Dangerous Hope had already cycled into False Hope. I just kept on coming up with reasons to justify why I wasn't seeing the proof on paper.

Over the next twenty months, that was the inner monologue I played over and over again. When I would have coughing attacks, I called it a spiritual attack. When I lost weight because of malnutrition from not being able to absorb nutrients because cystic fibrosis was still actually a part of my DNA, I made the decision to only allow enzymes back in my routine so I could stay at a healthy weight. I figured that the thing I really prayed for was my lungs to be healed of CF. I didn't actually pray for my digestive system to be healed of CF. As long as I could breathe, I didn't care if I had to take pills to absorb nutrients. So yes, the pills I flushed down the toilet eventually became pills I picked up from the pharmacist again. I compromised. But I drew the line at getting the breathing medicine again. I "flushed" those in the garbage that day in 2010, searing the decision in my mind, and I was never returning to that old life!

INSPECTING MY WEEDS

You can laugh here. I know you might want to. It's ridiculous the things we come up with to justify False Hope. They don't make sense, really. But when our Dangerous Hope starts to have setbacks, we fall into wishing, manifesting positive proof, and justifying things that we are supposed to actually face and confront. False Hope is tricky like that. It toes the line between fantasy and reality.

Since I inspected the seeds that I planted in the last chapter, it is good to also inspect the weeds that popped up during this False

Hope season. See if you can identify any of these weeds in your fields where the pesky perennial weed of False Hope might be residing:

THE WEED OF DENIAL: This is a tricky one to identify because it sometimes looks like a seed of faith or even a seed of positive thinking. It's important to realize that you don't have to refuse to acknowledge something in order to nourish the seeds of faith and a positive mindset. You can acknowledge the reality of a situation and still have faith that it will improve. You'll never find the weed of denial growing alone in a field. It likes to grow tall amidst other weeds like gossip, envy, a religious spirit, pride, ego, and lying, just to name a few. You know it's growing in your field when you feel the nudge to hide something, lie about it, refuse to acknowledge that you might not know enough about the situation to form an informed decision, or feel the urge to justify your decisions.

Clearly this weed was overtaking my field of hope. The medical documentation proved that CF was still very much a part of my DNA, but I was too busy justifying it by attributing it to that theory that sometimes things get worse before they get better. Uff da. It did not get better. In fact, the weed of denial was not eradicated until I started facing the facts and telling the truth — the truth about how I felt emotionally and spiritually, the truth about my actions, and the truth about what was happening in my body. That's how you start to eradicate the weed of denial. You face the truth. And then you begin problem solving and healing.

THE WEED OF FEAR: This weed is one of those weeds that could actually be put in a pretty pot and placed somewhere so you can see it every day as a visual reminder of courage. It's tricky because it's not necessarily a bad thing when it is found in your field. In fact, you won't ever be able to fully eradicate it; it serves a valuable purpose. You see, the weed of fear is actually the most important component in planting the seeds of courage. Without it, there is no courage because there is nothing to overcome and be brave about. We need the weed of fear to some extent, so we can feel the fear and do it, anyway. However, it becomes a problem when we feed the fear and let it infest our hearts. The weed of fear grows amidst the weeds of reasons, excuses, worry, and doubt. Anytime you focus on the worry and doubt, or you have to justify your fears with reasons and excuses why you can't overcome it, you've allowed this weed to overtake your field.

Here's the funny thing about how this weed showed up in my life at this time. I was not afraid of dying from my choice and lack of medication. Nope. I was afraid of letting God down and not having enough faith to follow through. On the one hand, my hope of God's miraculous powers was stronger than my fear of this disease. However, on the other hand, my fear of not having enough faith to stick it out and see a miracle was clouding my vision. I had to eradicate my fear by admitting it; that's when I was able to see a new perspective and grow courage again.

THE WEED OF AVOIDANCE: This weed also grows amidst the weed of denial. It distracts you and keeps you busy so you never get around to tending the ground that actually needs to be dealt with. It also grows beside the weeds of people pleasing and a lack of boundaries. You'll know that the weed of avoidance is festering in your field when you feel worn out, distracted, unproductive, scattered, and uncomfortable in your own skin. It grows best in environments that are messy and cluttered, jam-packed schedules, relationships that are laced with tension and comparison, and bodies riddled with health challenges. It especially shows up if you are trying to plant the seeds of rest and relaxation — it will do everything in its power to grow thick and strong so you can't plant those seeds.

During this season of my life, I was avoiding the reality of living with cystic fibrosis for sure! But I was also avoiding my doctors. And really anyone that had an opinion or concern that didn't line up with my faith and what I was hoping for. Once I started leaning into the situations I was avoiding, the weed of avoidance started to die. However, it is one of those weeds that you have to constantly be on the lookout for. Its seeds blow into new seasons of our lives again and again. It is like a dandelion — pretty to look at sometimes, but still a weed that must be plucked out of our field so we can grow healthy and strong.

THE WEEDS OF PRIDE, LYING, MANIPULATION, AND IRRESPONSIBILITY:

These weeds will always grow together. They feed off of each other. Pride always wants to look like the smartest person in the room so it lies. Lying looks enticing at first, but it breeds manipulation because you'll have to stay one step ahead of your lies so people don't discover the truth. And all of these actions are irresponsible. It's a vicious cycle! And I'm here to tell you that you will never get to experience your hopes and dreams when these weeds are growing in your life. You've got to eradicate them. You've got to step up and sow the seeds of humility, honesty, integrity, and responsibility instead. That's how you eradicate these weeds — you pluck them out when you notice them and sow new seeds immediately.

I think all of these weeds were tangled up in my heart. My pride kept me from seeking wisdom. So, I lied to my doctors because I wanted to manipulate this healing. And because the weeds of pride, lying, and manipulation were so thick and scratchy, irresponsibility just started sprouting out of the sides of each of them like some weird growth on a stem. Or a thorn. Yuck.

All these weeds were scattered among the seeds. It's almost like they were nourished by the roots of False Hope that were deeply imbedded into my field of Dangerous Hope.

If you look up the synonyms of "False Hope" you'll find words like daydream, wishful thinking, and fantasy. Imagination is actually an important element of healthy development in kids. As I look back on my childhood, I see that I had a strong imagination. However, in my imagination, I desired to be free of this incurable disease. That desire didn't go away as an adult, instead, it manifested itself in new ways. I think False Hope looks a bit different now as an adult than it did as a kid.

False Hope shows up when we retreat to fiction and avoid doing the hard things. In this action, we trick ourselves into believing that what we are hoping for will just fall into our laps without doing the work to cultivate it. This is just wishful thinking.

False Hope shows up when we naively think that the first time we do something we will be great at it. We trick ourselves into believing that the process doesn't apply to us because our belief is bigger, so that must mean it will happen faster. The truth is, when this happens, our ignorance is showing. We've got room for growth here.

False Hope shows up constantly, and it tricks us into thinking everything is fine. It's all going to just work out with no work on our part. That's the worst part of False Hope — it lies. It's naively optimistic and completely ignorant.

FALSE HOPE AND FAITH

There's a popular story I've heard that goes something like this:

A man finds himself stranded in the ocean, clinging to a life raft. He prays for God to save him. Pretty soon a helicopter shows up and throws down a ladder. The pilot yells out to the man, "Grab the ladder and we'll bring you to shore!" The man looks up and yells back, "No thanks! I'm waiting for God to save me!"

So, the helicopter flies away.

Pretty soon a submarine emerges and the captain walks out and throws a rope to the man. "Grab the rope and I'll pull you in. You can hitch a ride with us to our next stop. We have food and water and medical supplies inside," he says. The man looks at him and says, "No thanks! I'm waiting for God to save me!"

So, the submarine submerges under water and continues on its way.

Then the Coast Guard shows up in a boat. They stop right beside the man and let down their ladder. "Swim to the ladder and climb up into our boat. We will take you home," says the boat captain. Once again, the man looks at him and says, "No thanks! I'm waiting for God to save me!"

So, the Coast Guard leaves.

And the man is all alone in the ocean again — bobbing in the water. Eventually he grows tired and sadly, he drowns.

When he gets to Heaven, he marches up to God and says, "Why didn't you save me? I was waiting for you to save me!"

And God replies, "I sent you a helicopter, a submarine, and the Coast Guard. You refused all of them. What did you expect would happen?"

I never liked that story… until now. Actually, I think I avoided the truth of that story. I wanted to experience a miracle that was void of practicality; however, that's not always how God works. I see that now.

The Bible actually speaks about hope often. There are hundreds of verses about hope — what happens when we lose it, what kind of hope we should hang onto, and what to do when we hear False Hope.

I realize that not everyone reading this has the same faith as I do. I would imagine a book about hope, written by a chick with cystic fibrosis, would draw readers from all kinds of backgrounds. If you're reading this book wondering how people can believe in God at all, I want to explain something. When faith is a priority in someone's list of values, it is a deeply personal thing. Faith is one of my highest core values - so much so that I have a tattoo on my right foot that says "Walk by Faith." It is faded, and it takes a little bit of faith to actually see the A and the I in the word faith. My husband keeps telling me to get it touched up, but I actually love the visual of it — needing faith to see faith. It fits.

For people who hold faith in high esteem and strive to live a Godly life, walking by faith and not getting tripped up by False Hope can be a delicate dance at times. Feeding your faith can often look silly or downright stupid to those on the outside looking in. Honestly, it can sometimes feel as foolish as it looks at times.

For those of us who do believe in God, False Hope can show up when we choose to walk by faith toward something but forget that our Creator is also a very practical God. He likes to mix things up. Occasionally he might miraculously provide healing that leaves medical doctors scratching their heads, and the next several hundred times he might provide it through the people he created and with medicine. It's not for us to decide, actually. That's not faith; that's control, and we are not in control.

The election of 2020 was a great example of what it looks like when False Hope and Faith are intertwined. Many prophetic voices and leaders in the Evangelical world were prophesying that President Trump would be voted in for a second term. Now, this is a very heated topic, so I need to give a disclaimer here: No matter what you believe about that election, I encourage you to take a deep breath and stay with me here. There's wisdom to be gleaned about what it looks like when False Hope creeps in and we need to know how to handle this.

I recently watched a video of a woman that was in Washington D.C. to protest the inauguration of President Biden on January 20, 2021. In the video, she holds up a yellow sign that says, "Jesus Saves." The journalist asks her why she is there and she states that she is there because she believes that by God's supernatural power Donald J. Trump would remain the President of the United States. When the journalist lets her know that President Biden had just taken the oath to become the next president, she calmly states that it's okay because he will not take the power. The journalist continues to point out that President Biden had just been sworn in. You can hear a crowd cheering in the background as he becomes the president. The woman continues to insist that he cannot be president because he's not God's president. The journalist says, "but he is the President of the United States." And the woman stands firm in her belief and simply says, "no."

Now, the fact is that yes, President Biden did become President that day. Her False Hope was blinding her from seeing the facts. I don't know this woman personally, don't even know where she is from, but I can't help but wonder how she is now handling the letdown. For some people, False Hope and Faith entanglements that end in disappointment can cause them to doubt God, or even walk away from him, forever.

One of the Bible verses on False Hope is very applicable in this situation. The NIV of Jeremiah 23:16 says this: "This is what the Lord Almighty says: Do not listen to what the prophets are prophesying to you; they fill you with False Hopes. They speak visions from their own minds, not from the mouth of God." My friend, I know what it's like to want something on a spiritual level so much that you throw all of your hope into that outcome. I have wondered again and again if I truly heard from God the day I threw my medicine away or if I was "speaking a vision from my own mind." Just like God often uses medicine to heal people, he uses circumstances and even people that we don't like (such as politics or politicians) to accomplish new things on the earth. We can proclaim things all we want to but at a certain point if it's not coming to fruition, we need to confront reality and start asking ourselves how to move forward when things don't go our way. Sometimes our False Hope is more rooted in what we want than what God wants. We need to be willing to confront that and repent when we've pushed our own agendas no matter how good our intentions were.

"But Mandy, what about that verse in the Bible that says to speak those things that are not as though they are?"

If you're bringing that up, then you're probably referring to Romans 4:17. The NIV of that verse says this, "As it is written: I have made you a father of many nations (referring to Abraham). He is our father in the sight of God, in whom he believed — the God who gives life to the dead and calls things that are not as though they were." Context is always important when it comes to reading and understanding the Bible. And I will one hundred percent agree that it is important to speak faith and be intentional with our words because our words are powerful. Our words can build someone up or tear them down, and we should be aware of them and choose them wisely. However, we must also understand that living out the values in the Bible can sometimes be filled with complexities that are not easily explained quickly.

Walking by faith does not mean you speak something and it appears out of thin air like a magic trick. When hope and faith are truly grounded in God, it means that you trust him enough to let go of controlling the outcome and the timeline of the things you are praying for. If you're wrestling with this entire part of the chapter, I encourage you to dive into your Bible and ask God to speak to your heart and give you understanding. Ask him to show you where False Hope and Faith has become entangled, keeping you stuck from moving forward. You are not meant to stay trapped in the ignorance and confusion of False Hope.

And if you're reading this, scoffing at the whole faith and God idea, then take this section as a chance to learn how other people think and understand them maybe a little bit better than you did before. There's room for all of our viewpoints, and chances are you actually have faith in something, even if you don't have faith in God or a religion. You might have faith in science, faith in the universe, or even faith in people. Faith is described as a "confidence or trust in a person or thing," and a "belief that is not based on proof." From those definitions, we can agree that all hypotheses we have in life are first founded on a belief that has yet to be based on proof. Chances are, the wisdom shared in this section can still apply to you. Look at your own faith experience and find the False Hope moments within it. I guarantee there's some sort of personal growth opportunity for you in your own journey of hope.

FALSE HOPE DURING A PANDEMIC

False Hope has been creeping around ever since Covid-19 entered our reality. I'm not sure what it has been like in your part of the world, but here in North Dakota many people have faced this pandemic by simply deciding it's not that serious. Oh, we all took it seriously when this first started. But now, almost a year later, we are weary and tired of this reality.

I get it. I'm weary and tired of it too! It's hard to know when you should wear a mask and when you shouldn't, when you should stay home and when it is okay to go out. Personally, when I am with my co-workers at both my part-time job and at the office with my business partner, I don't wear a mask. We stay away from each other if we've been sick; we quarantine if we've been around someone that tested positive; we social distance and stay a safe distance apart, and if it gets a little crowded in the common areas, I remove myself and go to a room alone or just put more space between us. It's what I've had to do around other CFers over the last few decades so it isn't hard for me. However, I always wear a mask when I'm out in public and there are crowds of people around. Not just because it has been mandated in most businesses, but because it gives me anxiety if I don't. I've gone the entire pandemic this way and have yet to catch Covid-19.

Just the other day I went to a large church service — the second time in a year, mind you. My husband and I wore our masks and socially distanced, but honestly, we were two of only a handful that did. In a crowd of almost 1,000 people, many were acting as though the pandemic was gone and life is back to normal. For someone who has learned the hard way why science and faith need to learn to collaborate, this was disheartening.

The speaker that day was none other than the world-renowned John C. Maxwell. He was in town for his *Change Your World* Book Tour with co-author, Rob Hoskins. I found it somewhat ironic that he talked about social trust. Here's what he said:

> "Social trust is the confidence that other people will do what they ought to do."

I had to chuckle because sitting in a crowded sea of maskless people during a pandemic didn't exactly instill social trust in my heart. I've lived with the tension of being a high-risk person and still trying to find ways to be social during this pandemic. Had I never experienced what I did from my decision to throw away my medication, I probably would act the exact same way, actually. But I know what it's like to ignore science and medicine — to pretend that the reality of a disease is not real. I know what it's like to struggle to breathe and I really don't want to experience that again anytime soon. Nor do I want to inadvertently spread the virus to someone who might experience struggling to breathe. It's a horrible sensation that I wouldn't wish on my worst enemy.

One of the things I have yet to mention is how my medical team has had to approach me in a doctor's room. For the last several years, because of the increased risk of contracting deadly bacteria, the Cystic Fibrosis Foundation has mandated that all medical staff must be fully gowned up and masked anytime that they are treating a cystic fibrosis patient. This means that they wear a mask and a plastic coat-like sheet when they enter my room. When they leave, they throw it all away. If they reenter, they grab a new set and go through the whole crinkly-noised process all over again. It's been that way for years. I used to get irritated that they expected me to wear a mask as well. I hated being treated like I was sick or at such a risk of infection! But then the pandemic came around and the irritation turned into a deep sense of gratitude.

At my last CF checkup day, I had a conversation with a few of the people on my medical team about how to handle living in the pandemic while also living with cystic fibrosis. I brought up the fact that I had sat in that church auditorium the previous weekend and was quite honestly shocked that so few people were wearing masks. We sat across from each other in chairs — my doctor gowned and masked up. Through my masked face I told her that I was getting lonely from isolating myself from larger gatherings and I just needed some guidance on how to know what's safe. I shared how I knew of a teenager with CF in another town that hadn't even been around his friends for nearly a year. She assured me that precautions are still very necessary, but that it also wasn't good for mental health to isolate so severely.

That's been the challenge of living with cystic fibrosis during a pandemic. The good news is that Covid-19 infection numbers within the CF community are way better than originally predicted. Why is that? Because the CF community is full of rock stars that know how to mask up and social distance. We've had to practice this for decades now. And yet, many people will still fight me on the fact that masks help.

The state that I live in had a scary rise in Covid-19 cases in the Fall of 2020. The North Dakota Department of Health took it upon themselves to update our state daily on their Facebook page. According to an infographic that they posted on November 14th, 2020 our daily totals looked like this:

- 11,311 Active Cases
- 2,278 Daily New Positive Test Results
- 305 Currently Hospitalized
- 17.1% Daily Positivity Rate

Our state finally made a state-wide mask mandate after that. Large crowd church services went back to online services only for about a month and a half, and then right before Christmas, they came back full-swing. The mask mandate was lifted in the middle of January 2021. What was the result of that mandate? Take a look at the numbers that the North Dakota Department of Health posted on February 4, 2021:

- 921 Active Cases
- 155 Daily New Positive Test Results
- 37 Currently Hospitalized
- 2.3% Daily Positivity Rate

Turns out, the mask mandate worked. Our cases decreased. But now that the mask mandate has been lifted, so many people are walking around in crowds of people not doing what they "ought to do" because what we ought to do is inconvenient and uncomfortable. So, we tell ourselves that what we ought to do doesn't really make a difference. And we ignore the scientific proof that it helped.

False Hope does that; it will make you forget that the reason something improved is because of the hard work you put into it prior to that result. It will make you think that it was all just magic, and now you can stop doing the thing that created the positive result. False Hope in a pandemic is a scary thing because it risks the most precious thing on the planet: real human lives.

FALSE HOPE AND TOXIC POSITIVITY

In his book, *Man's Search for Meaning*, Viktor E. Frankl details the horrific events of living in Nazi death camps during World War II. While describing his first time entering a concentration camp he says,

> "In psychiatry there is a certain condition known as "delusion of reprieve." The condemned man, immediately before his execution, gets the illusion that he might be reprieved at the very last minute. We, too, clung to shreds of hope and believed to the last moment that it would not be so bad."

Pages later he goes on to explain,

> "Many times, hopes for a speedy end to the war, which had been fanned by optimistic rumors, were disappointed. Some men lost all hope…"

False Hope and Toxic Positivity go hand in hand. When we flippantly throw around positive statements without fully embracing the reality of a tough situation, we damage our ability to be prepared for the possibility of horrific outcomes. While a tough book to read, *Man's Search for Meaning* gives you a glimpse of traumatic situations and will surely give you a different perspective to consider.

"But Mandy, I thought it was good to be positive!"

Yes, it is. But there comes a point where being positive actually does some harm if it dismisses feelings and keeps you from confronting real issues that need to be addressed in order to experience the positive outcome you hope for. In an online article from *Psychology Today*, it is explained like this:

"The phrase "toxic positivity" refers to the concept that keeping positive, and keeping positive only, is the right way to live your life. It means only focusing on positive things and rejecting anything that may trigger negative emotions. But that sounds pretty good, right? Not so fast.

When you deny or avoid unpleasant emotions, you make them bigger. Avoiding negative emotions reinforces this idea: Because you avoid feeling them, you tell yourself that you don't need to pay attention to them. While you are trapped in this cycle, these emotions become bigger and more significant as they remain unprocessed. But this approach is simply unsustainable. Evolutionarily, we as humans cannot program ourselves to only feel happy.

By avoiding difficult emotions, you lose valuable information."

I've been known to fan the flames of toxic positivity myself in the past. That's what we do when we don't know any better. We do this as a means to help encourage someone else; to help them or ourselves see that there's always something to be thankful for — there's always something good. And while that is true, it is a bit more complicated than that. Facing our difficult emotions is important. It is a necessary part of The Cycle of Dangerous Hope.

When it comes to mental health, dismissing difficult emotions is very damaging. However, people do this every day without realizing it. It sounds like this,

"You don't need to worry about your weight — I wish I looked like you and had your problems!"

"I'm sorry you feel that way, but you really shouldn't."

"What are you worrying about? You've got a roof over your head and food on the table — your life is great compared to someone living in a third world country!"

Toxic positivity phrases like that push people away from you. They close the door on vulnerability and only spread more isolation, shame, and guilt. We need to learn how to handle our difficult emotions — how to identify them, process them, and move through them in a healthy manner. Our mental health depends on it. So does Dangerous Hope. It won't happen overnight. There are still times where I fall into the old habit of slapping on a toxic, positive mantra instead of leaning into the vulnerability of a difficult emotion for myself or others. It takes practice. I've gotten so much better at identifying False Hope and Toxic Positivity in my own life, but I know there's more room to grow. One of the ways I keep growing in this area is by meeting with a counselor each month. Brittany Schank, owner of Solace Counseling in Fargo, ND has been a Godsend to me in the lonely months of this pandemic.

Chances are you, or someone you know, have been struggling to keep a positive perspective since we entered the pandemic. You've probably been stuffing your feelings and giving into toxic positivity without realizing it, thinking that you were helping and not realizing that it is one of the reasons you're feeling hopeless. According to an article from *Business.com*, "The circumstances created by the spread of Covid-19 and the national response to the pandemic have impacted the vast majority of employees. Nearly 70% of American workers reported that the Covid-19 pandemic has been the most stressful time of their career. Similarly, 88% of employees reported moderate to extreme stress in the early months of the pandemic."

While coaching and leadership training is not the same as counseling, the skills learned from leadership training can help you cope better with the stresses of the pandemic. I highly encourage you to find a counselor, or even a Life or Leadership Coach, to help you grow in this area, too.

•••

Since the original idea for this Dangerous Hope concept was birthed from a fictional world — *The Hunger Games* — it should come as no surprise that the False Hope concept was first brought to my attention in a similar fashion. One night, a few months before the pandemic began, I was home alone watching *The Vampire Diaries*. In season eight, episode twelve, a character named Kade makes this statement, "I wouldn't want to give you False Hope." I quickly pushed pause and made a note of his quote in my phone, followed by the question, "where does False Hope fit in?"

It's funny that a character like Kade — described as the devil in this season — would make a comment about False Hope when the entire Vampire Diaries world is filled with False Hope situations such as people dying, turning into vampires, dying as vampires, and eventually coming back from the dead again as vampires. It's a wildly wicked ride that will have your emotions twisted in knots of anxiety in every episode!

This chapter has been the hardest one to write. It's 2:40pm on a Friday afternoon and I've been writing this chapter since 7:30am. I took a break to eat and get a few errands out of the way, but overall, I've been wrestling with this chapter all day long. When I first started writing this chapter back in December, it felt like it could be the fluffiest chapter in the book. Now that it's almost complete, I realize that the resistance to write it has been because the truth about it is offensive. Please know that my goal in this chapter was never to offend anyone, although I'm not in charge of whether or not you sit in offense. That's your responsibility to deal with. But the concepts shared around the weeds of False Hope are uncomfortable to face when we look in the mirror. It stirs the pot of our vulnerability whether we are ready to confront it or not. Like Kade from *The Vampire Diaries*, I would never want to give you False Hope. I think that's why sharing my story of believing for a healing of cystic fibrosis and living out the reality of it has been so hard for me to tell. Never would I ever want to give another cystic fibrosis patient False Hope and encourage them to throw away their medication. That's so dangerous. And yet the False Hope that I walked in brought me to writing this book. Probably because you needed these words more than either of us knew.

In January 2012, I found myself in Orlando, Florida for another conference. False Hope had run its course and was slowly morphing into Hope Deferred. The entire weekend was a struggle. My body was exhausted and my lungs felt heavy. I didn't know it at the time, but I was battling a very bad case of bronchitis. I carried a little bottle of peppermint essential oil in my purse and huffed it several times a day because it was the only thing that helped me breathe and kept the anxiety attacks at bay.

On the second day of the conference, I considered skipping it and sleeping instead. One of my roommates, Elise, did her best to encourage me to get up and get dressed. She bribed me with a Starbucks latte, reminding me that if I just found the strength to put myself together, I could enjoy a venti caramel macchiato and learn about personalities. It worked. I mustered up all of my strength, put my hair into a messy bun and got myself down to the conference. And then I spent the majority of the personalities session in the bathroom huffing that bottle of peppermint essential oil because the struggle to breathe was like nothing I had experienced before. I barely remember flying home two days later; I just recall that it was an excruciating trip where it felt like my lungs and my legs were trudging through peanut butter.

I got home and went to the doctor — a different doctor at a totally different hospital. One that had no experience with me or cystic fibrosis. They put me on an antibiotic for bronchitis and I went on my way. In a week I was feeling much better. But slowly, day by day, the decline got worse and disappointment settled in.

That's how you know it's time to work the mulch of Hope Deferred into the ground — when your soil is ripe with disappointment.

That's how you know it's time to work the mulch of Hope Deferred into the ground — when your soil is ripe with disappointment.

FIVE
•••
The Mulch of Hope Deferred

The first time I ever remember experiencing Hope Deferred was as a freshman in high school. I tried out for All-State Choir and was certain I would make it in. What I failed to realize, however, was that my talent of singing by ear and emulating vocalists like Mariah Carey and Celine Dion wasn't exactly what they were looking for. In order to pass the audition, one had to be able to sight read sheet music and sing it on the spot. This was my epic downfall, and I botched the audition right then and there. I was absolutely crushed that I wasn't chosen. I cried for hours about it. In dramatic fashion I played a song by the Christian group Avalon over and over again as the soundtrack to my pity party. I poured out my heart to

God and reminded myself that the dreams God had for me were indeed bigger than the dreams I had for me.

I couldn't help but wonder — how could God's dreams be bigger than me becoming the next Celine Dion? My freshman heart couldn't fathom that. Nor would I have guessed that when I finally made it into the All-State Choir as a senior, I would decline the offer to enter a beauty pageant. I actually did win the beauty pageant. I mean, scholarship pageant. And while the experience helped with my stage presence, it did not land me the dream job of becoming the next Celine Dion.

Hope Deferred was something that I had gone through time and time again when my dreams didn't work out the way I thought they would. But the Spring of 2012 brought a new level of Hope Deferred. The lowest of lows that I had only ever seen in movies.

•••

Not quite two years after flushing my medication down the toilet, I found myself lying in bed at 30 years old, mentally preparing for what was about to happen. In a moment I would sit up and the coughing attack would begin.

First, mucus would clog my sinuses and lungs.

Then my palms and forehead would begin to drip with sweat.

My heart would race from the fear of suffocating.

I would crawl to the floor and sit in front of the fan. If I was lucky, I would have just enough energy to slowly walk to the fridge in the kitchen to get a cold bottle of water and then return to the spot on the floor in my bedroom. If I wasn't lucky, the lukewarm bottle of water that I had kept on my nightstand would have to suffice.

Then, I would start coughing uncontrollably and in between gasping for air, tell myself out loud, "You're okay." Gasp. "You're okay." Gasp. "You're okay." Gasp. If Nate was there, he would be my coach and tell me those words in a slow, calm voice. But he wasn't always there, and our fur baby Ajah B. certainly couldn't talk, so I had to learn to be my own coach.

This coughing/panic/anxiety attack would last approximately twenty minutes. I would cough so hard I threw up mucus and bile. My body would be drenched in sweat by the time I was done, and I'd be so exhausted that I would want to go back to bed.

I had lost over twenty pounds by then and was averaging 98 pounds soaking wet. In an attempt to shift my perspective and find something good about this fact, I decided to celebrate and be grateful that I could finally wear a padded bra. As a larger busted young woman, cute padded bras were never anything I got to try out. But now, my once very curvy bust had shrunk down to thin, sagging sacks that I didn't recognize. A padded bra wasn't just something to celebrate, it was needed to hide the emaciation.

My body was so frail and bony that I had to sit on a towel when I took a bath because without the extra padding for my bony butt, it was too painful. If I pinched my calves between my fingers, I could actually feel my fingers touching through the skin. My body was so malnourished that it was absorbing every ounce of fat and muscle that it could find to try and stay alive. I walked around hugging myself in self-protection because even a simple hug from someone would physically hurt.

Nate worked in the oil field at the time, and would be gone for two weeks and then home for two weeks. The weeks he was gone went by fast and slow at the same time. Much of that time was spent sleeping. Sometimes I would be so frail and exhausted that I would just sleep in the hallway because I didn't have the energy to get to the couch or the bed. Ajah B. was my loyal companion back then, always curling up by me and keeping watch over me. I'm convinced the only reason she was saved from our apartment fire is so that she could give me a reason to live when I needed it most. Without her there with me, it would have been much easier to just give in to the constant desire to sleep the world away and let go of what little hope I tried to hold on to.

I was fading away and everyone could see it. But I was so stuck in Hope Deferred that I didn't know how to dig myself out of the hell I had put myself in. I had become the villain of my own story.

That was the beginning of March 2012.

At some point during that month, my mom came to town to take care of me while Nate was at work. I don't think she was fully prepared for what she was about to encounter. I had lost more weight, and I was still going through the regulation period of getting used to anti-depressants, so my mood was a far cry from the optimistic daughter she was used to seeing and hearing.

The first night she was there, I spent a good hour in my bathroom in a coughing fit that turned into a panic attack. I turned the fan on to try and mask the sound, but it didn't help. She spent that night listening to me suffer, praying and calling my dad trying to figure out how to help me. I'm sure she was terrified at the thought of losing me.

The next morning, I woke up to my mom calmly walking into my room and letting me know that my dad had called my doctor and she was going to take me to the hospital. I was furious. The day before we had a heart-to-heart chat where she talked me into getting medical help. I had told her that Nate and I would call the doctor and go in when he got back from work. Listening to me struggle to breathe all night caused her to take matters into her own hands. Looking back now, I don't blame her. However, at the time I felt that my wishes were not honored and I resented the fact that my parents didn't let me take care of things on my terms. I was a grown woman, after all!

With sun shining through my bedroom patio door, I snuggled in my blankets, cuddling with Ajah B., and sent the following text to my best friend, Raychel:

"Okay. How. Old. Am. I? Because my mom just came in and said she's taking me to the hospital like I'm a kid again."

Raychel was three months pregnant with her third child, and at that very moment, she was driving on a busy street with her second child, a toddler at the time, in the back seat. She saw the text message and pulled over into a Wendy's parking lot because at first glance, she thought to herself, "Oh my god, how medicated is she that she doesn't remember how old she is?! Something is seriously going down with my bestie!"

I went on to explain that yes, I knew I was 30 years old and that my text message was a rhetorical question because I was so flustered at the treatment I was getting from my mom. I asked Raychel if I could spend the night on her big blue couch until Nate could come home, and she graciously agreed and said she was on her way to pick me up. So, while my mom was in the shower getting ready for the day, I packed my purse full of oranges for snacks, put on my pink bathrobe, tucked my dog under my arm, and ran away from my own house through the patio door in my bedroom. I left my mom a note thanking her for coming to take care of me, but asking her to please go home.

I didn't talk to my parents for two months after that. It was the darkest time of my life, and theirs.

Now, there's probably a lot of questions swimming in your head after reading that. You're probably wondering… why the oranges? Next you might be wondering… why didn't you get dressed, Mandy? And, finally you're probably asking… how could you do that to your mom?

I get it. This part of the story can only be summed up in one word: crazy. My bestie and I actually laugh often about this part of the story because what 30-year-old-woman runs away from her own house in her bathrobe with her purse packed full of oranges? Who does that?!

A 30-year-old-woman on the brink of a mental breakdown, that's who!

For real. Mental health issues are not something to joke about, however this part of my story deserves some giggles because sometimes the only way to get through the crazy is to laugh. And my actions were exactly the kind of thing you would see in a movie like *Girl, Interrupted* or *Silver Linings Playbook*.

During the first four months of 2012, I craved oranges in a crazy way. My stomach had shrunk because of how little I was eating, and I was barely hungry from the flight or fight response happening in my body with all the constant panic attacks. I practically lived on oranges though, so I ate them nearly around the clock. It's become a funny inside-joke with Raychel and me now; an inside-joke that we use as a signal to ask the deeper question of "are you really okay?" After doing some research, I learned that the vitamin C in oranges actually helps lower cortisol levels. Cortisol is the stress hormone, and during anxiety and panic attacks, cortisol levels can get to super high levels. Apparently craving oranges was my body's way of trying to lower the stress levels it was experiencing.

As to why I didn't get dressed when I ran away from home — I don't have an answer for that. None at all. I do know that making simple decisions like what to wear or what to eat felt extremely hard during that timeframe. I'm guessing just embracing my hot-mess-self was the best I could do in that moment. Plus, I was totally hopped up on anti-depressants and anxiety medication. I couldn't even.

Now let's talk about running away from home. My mom is one of the sweetest women on the planet. Every month for the first 20 years of my life she was the one that diligently drove me to doctor appointments. Our mother-daughter bonding moments were plentiful because of those trips. We even met every Tuesday night on her couch to watch *Gilmore Girls* together. She would make her delicious popcorn — with the white kernels and the yummiest melted butter and just the right amount of salt — and we would laugh and cry and tell our husbands to be quiet when they couldn't understand the fast-talking dialogue. So of course, it broke my heart to run away from her like that. And I know that it also broke hers. My only explanation for this is that I felt threatened and forced into something that I was not ready to handle without my husband by my side. Since I was in a constant state of fight or flight, it's no wonder I felt like fleeing from my own mother was my only option.

I lived on Raychel's big blue couch for the next few days waiting for Nate to come back from work. I blocked my parents' numbers from my phone. Actually, I blocked most family members from my phone. I couldn't handle their worry and fear without experiencing rapid panic attacks and weight loss. It was the only healthy boundary I could think of to stop the physical symptoms from devouring me. In the middle of the night with Ajah B. snuggled up by my feet on the big blue couch, I prayed that God would be with my parents. I prayed that God would comfort them in their fears and in the pain that I was inevitably causing them.

And I prayed God would keep them safe from harm. My biggest fear was that they would die before we had a chance to reconcile. Which is ironic, because their biggest fear was that *I* would die before we had a chance to reconcile. Their fear was way more likely of becoming a reality than mine was.

When Nate got home from his week on the rig, we went to the clinic. The actual CF Clinic this time. If I remember right, my lung functions that day were at 50%, a number they had stayed stable at for about a year (which I only know because I eventually went back to the doctor one other time before this in 2011). My doctors recognized the fragile mental state I was in, and didn't push for me to be in the hospital for a tune-up. Instead, they told me to come back in a month and to keep track of where things were at. I agreed that I could do that, even though I told them I would not do breathing treatments again. I'm bullheaded like that.

Things declined rapidly from there.

The next month, at the end of April 2012, Nate and I went on a trip to Duluth, Minnesota. We had never been there, and we were excited to spend a few days in a cozy cabin on the shores of a lake so enormous it felt like an ocean. It was supposed to be a wonderful, somewhat romantic trip. I barely remember it. What I do remember, is being so frail that Nate had to carry me most places, and sleeping. A lot.

Panic attacks were an around the clock thing at this point, and not even a cocktail of Zoloft and Xanax could keep them at bay anymore. On the drive home, the truck wheels rolled over some very loud and bumpy road strips and I had to have Nate pull over because it caused such a panic attack that I couldn't catch my breath.

I'll never forget the night I gave in and gave up the fight. We were sitting on our couch watching a very violent movie. In my mind, I was fighting with myself. On one hand I wanted to stay strong and keep the hope of a miraculous healing alive. On the other hand, I was wasting away and I wasn't sure I could survive another two weeks alone without someone to take care of me when Nate went to work. I didn't know for sure, but it felt like I was dying. And then an explosive, graphic scene happened in the movie that I did not expect and I was in a full-blown panic attack where I couldn't breathe. I told Nate that I couldn't do this anymore. I had to go to the hospital in the morning and get medical intervention.

You might be wondering how my husband could let me get to this point. This is where I need to let you know that Nate was doing his best to be a supportive husband and honor my wishes during this time. There were a lot of people — family members and medical professionals and friends — that were trying desperately to get me the help I clearly needed. I'm sure many of them prayed for me to come to my senses. And I'm so thankful that they did. However, this was my choice, and nobody could save me from it but me. My husband understood that. He also saw first-hand the physical toll that the fears and worries of family members had taken on me. He understood why I blocked everyone on my phone and on social media. He didn't want to add to that stress, so he did everything he could to honor my choice.

Nate was also hoping for the miracle to be real. And while I can't speak for him, I have to admit that I didn't put him in an easy position. But I'm so thankful that he honored my wishes, both when I made a risky Dangerous Hope decision, and when I reached the end of that rope full of Hope Deferred and nearly wasting away because of it.

So, the next morning we called the clinic and told them I would be coming in to be admitted. They were ready for me, but they weren't mentally prepared for the condition they were about to see me in.

I nearly passed out from the breathing test. Me. The model patient that would hop on her stiletto heels to get every ounce of air out of her lungs during a breathing test couldn't even stand to finish it. I only did one breathing test that day. The numbers showed something I've never seen before — 22%. The Dangerous Hope that caused me to take drastic action had caused my lung functions to plummet.

They wheeled me up to my room in a wheel chair and hooked me up to oxygen right away. I was so frail and so full of panic that I couldn't even handle the vest portion of my breathing treatments for the first few days; the shaking of the vest was just too much for my mind and body to handle. Prior to this hospital stay, I had never been hooked up to oxygen. Now, it was a necessity around the clock.

My strength was so depleted that I even had to have the oxygen on when I took a shower, and my husband had to wash my hair for me because I didn't have the physical stamina to do even that simple task. His love and care for me in those hair-washing moments broke my heart for what he was going through and made me fall deeper in love with him at the same time.

Every medical person that walked into my room had tears in their eyes as they assessed me. Never in their wildest dreams did they think they would ever see me in this condition.

I never dreamed it either.

My medical team knew that I wasn't speaking to my parents, and I'm sure that made the whole situation even more heartbreaking for them. There was another CF patient — an older adult — that was in the hospital at the same time as I was. He was in his forties or fifties, and he passed away within a day or two of me getting to the hospital. My medical team went to his funeral and when they returned, they mentioned that they saw my parents there. Because of HIPPA laws, they couldn't say anything of course, but they let me know that my parents had talked to them. Apparently, my mom had been praying for me the morning I went into the hospital and she suddenly looked up at my dad and said, "Mark, I think Mandy is in the hospital." So, she called the hospital to find out what room I was in, and her premonition was confirmed. At this gentleman's funeral, my parents told my medical team that they knew I was in the hospital and my team reassured them that I was getting the best care possible.

During one of the first days there, one of my respiratory therapists gave me the gift of compassion when she came in and just let me cry in her presence. The room was dark, with nothing but a gray sky trying to peek through the shades. It matched my solemn mood and I welcomed it. Even now, almost a decade later, I can see my red-haired RT walking over to the chair to sit with me as I breathed in my treatment, tears streaming down my face. She didn't ask me to explain my emotions; she simply sat with me as I cried.

To this day I'm not exactly sure what I was crying about. It was probably a mixture of grief from everything that had and hadn't happened in my life over the last two years, along with the reality that cystic fibrosis was still very much in my body and there was nothing I could do about it. All I know is that I was so very sad and I felt completely abandoned by God.

Things began to turn around after four days of hospital care when one of my closest friends came to visit me. She didn't scold me or make me feel foolish for throwing all of my hope and faith into the decision that led me to this life-threatening situation. Instead, she lovingly reassured me that God wasn't mad at me and that it was perfectly fine to be allowing medical intervention back into my life. Her encouragement sparked hope in my heart again, and even though this friend has since chosen to leave my life, I'll be forever thankful for the grace and compassion she showed me in that moment.

Later that night, I dragged my frail 92-pound self out of bed and hobbled over to the bathroom sink, the oxygen tube snaking along with me. The face staring back at me in the mirror shocked me to my core. Gray skin, sunken-in cheeks, sad, fear-filled eyes. It reminded me of the look I had seen on the faces of my friends who had passed away from cystic fibrosis. This was the sickest version of myself that I had ever seen. I had taken a giant leap of faith when I flushed my medicine down the toilet that day in 2010, and it did not pan out the way I had hoped. There was nothing left to do now but own that decision and bravely walk out the consequences of it.

With fierce determination, and the voice of the coach I would one day become, I stared into my eyes in the mirror and said out loud, "Mandy, this is not how your story ends. No matter what your new normal is — whether that means wearing oxygen for the rest of your life, or having to take insulin shots for CF-related diabetes, or needing a feeding tube, or all of the above — no matter what, you will make this matter."

The next day my appetite returned. My lung function test that afternoon showed that I had improved from 22% to 44%. And by the end of the weekend, I was moved into a transitional care unit where I spent the next two weeks recovering. It was during this time that I texted my parents and told them I loved them, but I wasn't quite ready to see them or hear their voices. I'm not sure, but it's possible that this was my subconscious way of protecting them from seeing their only child so sick.

The transitional care unit was lonely. I missed my husband when he was working and I really missed my dog, Ajah B. Friends took care of her while Nate was on the oil rig. Once or twice, when

Nate was home, he brought Ajah B. to the hospital and my doctor let me go outside to see her. I'm sure my furry companion was so confused as to why I was there instead of at home with her.

I spent my days doing four treatments a day, eating as often as I could, goofing off with the nurses, and reading books. God felt distant still, and I was still processing my Hope Deferred feelings, so reading the Bible just didn't seem like something I could do. Instead, I found comfort in the pages of *The Hunger Games* trilogy. Katniss's experience with PTSD and anxiety was something I identified with and I had never read another story where it was described so well. This was the season of my life where I fell in love with story of *The Hunger Games*.

Eventually, I reconciled with my parents, and our relationship began to heal. And twenty-two days later I was able to go home. I weighed just over 100 pounds and my lung functions were at 69% the day I left.

The miracle of my story is not that I was miraculously healed of cystic fibrosis. The miracle of my story is that I lived to tell the tale, without needing a lung transplant, and my health has been fully restored. It has taken almost a decade, and a ton of diligence to my medicine and healthy lifestyle habits, but today my lung functions average between 79% to 83%. I have more energy than I have ever had before, and I am a runner. In the Fall of 2019, I ran my first ever half-marathon and I have a hunch it won't be my only one.

INSPECTING MY MULCH

It took me the entire summer of 2012 to start to feel like myself again — to work all of the mulch of Hope Deferred into the ground so I could be ready to sow the seeds of Dangerous Hope again. I call it my Picasso Period, because I spent a lot of time getting in touch with my creativity again. I painted a bunch of pictures to hang on the buttercup yellow walls of our apartment because we desperately needed artwork, and I desperately needed to express myself through art.

God still seemed far away, and I couldn't find the strength to dive into the Bible like I once had. Instead, I found him in the pages of Christian novels by one of my favorite authors, Karen Kingsbury. That summer I must have read ten of them, continuing the tradition I once had with my Grandma Agnes of dating the book and initialing it when I finished it. For a few years before she died, we would read those books, sign and date the first page when we were done, and mail them to each other. It was a precious tradition that meant more to me than words could express. Reading those novels during the summer of 2012 helped me feel close to God again, and it helped me process all of the loss I had experienced since Grandma passed away in 2009.

Just like I had to inspect the seeds of Dangerous Hope and the weeds of False Hope, I must inspect the mulch of Hope Deferred. You see, we need to have a good understanding of what our organic material is before we learn to work it into the ground. Our disappointments, our unmet expectations, our loneliness and hurt feelings from relationships — all of that is mulch. And if they just sit on the surface of our fields, like a pile of crap that can be stepped on, they do us no good. You won't grow anything beautiful from a pile of crap squished by a shoe. You'll just smear it everywhere you go and create a big mess. We've got to learn how to inspect the mulch of Hope Deferred so we can use it effectively. Here's the mulch that was ready to fertilize my soil, and how it might be ready to fertilize yours:

THE MULCH OF RESTORATION: Relationships are hard. In fact, in all the work I've done as a Life & Leadership Coach, conflict resolution and communication in relationships tend to be the topics that the majority of people struggle with. If you're struggling with a relationship right now, and hoping for restoration, be encouraged. You're not alone.

The mulch of restoration is messy. You won't be able to restore a relationship by glossing over the hurtful parts. You will have to come to terms with all of it in order to restore it. First, you'll have to be brave enough to admit that you are even hurt at all. You will have to be willing to look in the mirror and admit the actions you took that contributed to the problems. You will have to be willing to look at the situation from the other person's point of view and consider what they might be feeling. Restoration will demand healthy boundaries and new behaviors. It takes maturity and honesty. It takes forgiveness. And it often means working with a third party — like a counselor or a coach — so you have an unbiased point of view asking the right questions in order to facilitate effective conversations. But know this: Not every relationship is able to be restored — that takes two individuals who are willing to do the hard work. In the instances where abuse is happening on any level, restoration might not ever be possible or safe. In those instances, the mulch of restoration needs to be worked in the ground so you can be the one that is restored.

I wrestled with telling the part of my story where I asked my mom to go home and I stopped talking to my parents. It's a part of our history that is very hurtful for all of us, and I didn't want to say the wrong thing or make my parents look bad. I love my parents so much and I'm so thankful that they are my parents. But then I realized that I couldn't not tell it. Because maybe there are parents out there who need to know that restoration is possible. Maybe there are patients out there who have had to put similar boundaries up and didn't know anyone else who understood. I know my parents meant well. And I know that my reasons for blocking them and not talking to any of my extended family members weren't because I didn't love them or I was mad at them. It was because I didn't know what else to do to gain control of my anxiety and panic attacks. There were a lot of lessons I had to learn about boundaries, and I also had to go through a lot of counseling sessions to be able to process everything, so by no means do I want to paint the picture that restoration was easy. It took work. And now, my parents and I have a better understanding of each other and we don't take it so personally anymore when we see things differently.

THE MULCH OF REMAINING FAITH: The other day I saw a post on Twitter that said, "One of the great mistakes made by much of American Christianity is neglecting to prepare people for the dark night of the soul. Far too often people enter into this wilderness assuming they've lost their faith, rather than hearing an invitation to grow deeper." It's true. So often we start to lose faith when we pray for something and it doesn't happen. We fail to recognize the purpose of the darkness of Hope Deferred. Working in the mulch of remaining faith is hard. You will question if you had faith at all. You will question if it's worth it to keep having faith. Yes — it is worth it — keep the faith. Working in the mulch of remaining faith means giving yourself permission to wrestle with God. Be honest about your let downs. Go on a bike ride or a walk or a run and yell at the sky if you need to! God can handle your emotions. In fact, I think he actually really likes it when we are comfortable enough with him to show him all the sides of our emotions — the good, the bad, and the ugly.

If you don't have faith in God or religion, working in the mulch of remaining faith means giving yourself permission to wrestle with yourself. Question yourself. Let your paradigms shift as you grow and learn. Recognize where you started to lose faith and why, and then ponder the deeper growth that happened because of it. The mulch of remaining faith is an invitation to grow deeper, and to learn how to be content in the moments where your faith is hanging on by a thread.

I got the tattoo on my foot that says, "Walk by faith," after my season of Hope Deferred. That summer actually. I got it as a reminder that I still have faith. Sometimes my faith is small, because the bittersweet taste of taking a leap of faith and falling flat on my face still lingers on my tongue. However, my faith remains. And even if I have faith that is big enough to ask for something that I don't receive, I know that it is okay. My faith is actually grounded in the fact that God is who he says he is. That's what really matters when it comes to faith.

THE MULCH OF UNDERSTANDING SOMETHING BETTER: In every journey of Dangerous Hope, there will be something you think you understand, but you actually don't. This is where the mulch of understanding something better comes in. If you think you understand a situation or a person, but you've never seen the dark side of it, my friend, you do not yet understand it well enough. There is a dark side to everything — people, business, leadership, dreams, disease, relationships, everything. The dark side shows up when things don't go well, when trauma happens, or when hopelessness sets in. Most people try to hurry up and move on from those instances. Those are the people that have not worked the mulch of understanding something better into their field. From this point forward, you can't afford to be that person. You must lean in to the uncomfortableness of working in the mulch of understanding something better. Ask the hard questions. Settle into the dark side with someone without trying to fix them. Glean the wisdom that is ripe for the taking.

My mulch of understanding something better was this: Understanding the severity of cystic fibrosis. Prior to being so sick and nearly dying, I had no clue how horrible this disease was. Yes, I had read the stories and met people who were sicker than I was. Yes, I had friends who passed away from this disease. However, the sickest I ever got before flushing my medication was a lung function of 85%. And let me tell you, that's a breeze! That's close to where I'm at today and it's pretty great actually! But struggling to breathe... being so malnourished that it physically hurts... and experiencing the anxiety that comes from your body no longer working right... that's difficult. I'm so thankful that I understand it now and that I got to have my health restored.

I'm so thankful I experienced the dark side and lived to tell about it. It helps me advocate better.

You can't skip working the mulch of Hope Deferred into your soil. Not if you are serious about planting the seeds of Dangerous Hope and seeing them grow. The mulch of Hope Deferred takes on more forms than what I shared above. Sometimes it looks like the mulch of trauma, or the mulch of divorce, or the mulch of grieving a loved one that has died. Hope Deferred settles in and it will last longer than it should if we aren't intentional about it. But when you find the courage to get back up again, and you work that mulch of Hope Deferred into your ground, you will see new growth. It happens every time because that is how The Cycle of Dangerous Hope works.

This is usually the place where people get stuck, so before we end our time together in this chapter, I want to give you a bit more insight on Hope Deferred. You will need to know what it looks like in other instances and how to make sense of it. There are important skills you'll need to build in order to process it effectively as you work the mulch into your soil.

HOPE DEFERRED IN A PANDEMIC

I wish I could tell you that everything you hope for is going to happen quickly and with ease. Or that working the mulch of Hope Deferred into your ground will be a piece of cake. But that would be a lie. The hardest part of The Cycle of Dangerous Hope is recognizing what to do when the thing you hope for is delayed or it doesn't go like you thought it would. Reaping the lessons — that's the hard, yet very necessary part.

Biblical wisdom says that, "Hope Deferred makes the heart sick, but a longing fulfilled is a tree of life." (Proverbs 13:12, NIV)

The word "deferred" means "postponed or delayed."

Notice that it does not mean deleted or erased. Just delayed.

Everything the human race had been working for and hoping for came to a sudden halt in March 2020 when Covid-19 entered our reality. Events got cancelled, business revenue plummeted, schools shut down, and time just… paused. If the months of March, April, and May 2020 were represented as the pages of a book, they would be the empty pages of *New Moon* when Bella is going through depression. All of our longings were delayed, and it left us feeling empty in a way that made little sense.

According to an article published by the CDC on August 14, 2020, "Symptoms of anxiety disorder and depressive disorder increased considerably in the United States during April—June of 2020, compared with the same period in 2019."

Another source, published on June 4, 2020, stated that "48% of Americans are feeling down, depressed, or hopeless during the Covid-19 pandemic."

You might wonder, "What is the point of hope if the odds are always stacked against you?"

If you've been wondering that, you're not alone. I've felt that way too. There was a movie in the nineties called, *Hope Floats*, starring Harry Connick Jr. and Sandra Bullock. I actually did not like this movie back then; it seemed boring and sad. It's probably a movie I would glean wisdom and insight from now as an adult though. When you've been through some things, certain stories start to make more sense. But I'll be honest. I have had many moments when I doubted that hope floats at all. In fact, in my Hope Deferred moments, I often feel that hope blows right over you as you chase after it, looking like a fool.

A Google search of the phrase "feeling hopeless in the pandemic" brings a total of 2,700,000 results. If you've felt hopeless ever since the pandemic arrived, I want to reassure you that you're not alone. Remember in chapter two how I shared my experience of challenging my perspective when the pandemic first hit? In that chapter, I showed you how I shifted my perspective from a negative, self-pitying one to a more positive, empowering one. That example is exactly what it looks like to work the mulch of Hope Deferred into your field of hope.

In my experience, I've found that before I can work the mulch of Hope Deferred into the ground so it is fertile, I have to make sense of the hopeless feelings and the circumstances that led to those emotions. Making sense of Hope Deferred means sitting down with a cup of coffee, my journal, and my pen, and processing it all with strategic questions. I'll share the exact questions I use in the following section.

MAKING SENSE OF HOPE DEFERRED

A few months ago, I was listening to a podcast sermon from Elevation Church. The pastor, Steven Furtick, said this: "Burying your disappointment is not a sustainable strategy." Many people think the opposite is true. They are still holding on to the weeds of False Hope and Toxic Positivity that tell them to just stay positive and stuff the negative stuff away. However, that action only makes the seasons of Hope Deferred harder. Denying your disappointments only causes unnecessary delays and hurts.

I get it though. I actually used to be the kind of person that bottled up my disappointments and regrets, too. I would lock them into the darkest corners of my heart and I was the only one that knew where the key was. Then, on lonely nights, when the world was sleeping but my mind was wide awake, I'd tiptoe into the attic of my heart and hold those moments in my hand like a snow globe, staring at them. Trying to shrink myself into them again. Just for a moment. To finally make sense of what hurt and what was still affecting me even though I tried my damnedest not to let it.

In the pages of my twenty-eight journals from the last ten years, you'll find questions and answers and letters of how I wish things would have gone. What I would have said or done had I been able to. How I see things now, versus how I saw them, then.

Every time I wrote a story of how I wish it would've gone, I noticed something: A lesson was learned. Strength was gained, character built, and hope sparked again. Somehow, processing it in the pages of my journal helped me make sense of things so I could eventually move on and let go of the hopelessness I had locked within.

Burying our disappointments only holds us captive. It sabotages our relationships and stops us from growing and maturing. And, it kills our hope. Remember, hope is not a straight line from A to B. It is a cycle, and after we work the mulch of Hope Deferred into the ground, it should prepare the soil so we can sow more seeds of Dangerous Hope. That's what it *should* do. Our challenge is to get really good at going through the cycle and tilling the ground, so we keep Dangerous Hope growing. Hope is a long game and its constant opponent is disappointment.

My disappointments didn't end when I left the hospital after those twenty-two days. In fact, more disappointments were in the near future as I embarked on the journey of making it matter. However, rising out of the ashes of my circumstances in 2012 gave me strength. It built in me a resilience to be able to get really good at going through The Cycle of Dangerous Hope quickly so my Dangerous Hope could keep glowing.

I'm willing to bet that if you're reading these words, you've had disappointments in your life, too. And maybe you replay conversations, regrets, and disappointing moments over and over again in your mind, too. The bad news is that the only way to overcome this is to give yourself permission to process it all instead of locking it away. The good news is that this part of the book is your tool to do that.

If I were in a coaching session with you, I would ask you questions to help you process your thoughts and feelings. In the following sections you'll find the type of questions I would ask. They are crafted to help you look at different life moments to help you process what went down, how you wish it would have gone, and the lesson you learned because of it all — both the reality and the wish. Both points of view matter to your story in ways that will become clear once you follow through with the exercises. Take some time to answer the questions in the next three sections:

What happened was...

- What happened and who was involved?
- What was said that still haunts you today?
- What choices did you make then?
- What emotions did you feel at the time?

How I wish it would have gone...

- What do you wish you would have or could have said at the time?
- What do you wish they would have said?
- What do you wish they would have done?
- What choices do you wish you would have made instead?

How I see it now…

- What emotions are you feeling right now as you remember it all?
- How did this past situation shape you as a person today?
- How did this shape your thoughts about hope?
- What strength did you gain because of this that maybe you didn't realize you had until now?
- How has this experience affected your personal and professional relationships?
- What are three things you will choose to admire about the person or people involved in this past circumstance so you can feed gratitude instead of feeding bitterness and resentment?
- How can you take action to make this experience something that builds strength and hope instead of continuing to bury your disappointment?

The beautiful thing about this guide is you can apply it every time you start to feel hopeless, or you just want to gain some perspective. I must warn you though that the process of making sense of the Hope Deferred part of The Cycle of Dangerous Hope comes with complicated feelings. You might find yourself feeling simultaneously excited about a new opportunity and sad for the past. My counselor says this is perfectly normal. In fact, just the other day, during my monthly counseling session, she told me it was actually healthy to be able to hold both happy and sad emotions at the same time. When tough things happen in life, feeling both of those emotions at the same time is perfectly normal. The problem is that many people don't know how to process it. And that's why they stuff it away. However, from this point forward, you have this guide to process it. Which means you are equipped to handle this and grow stronger now.

Don't be afraid to wrestle with sparking hope again, my friend. This is your chance to disrupt the setbacks and rewrite the story in a way that matters to you, and eventually, to others.

In my experience of going through this process, I have learned that every time I am disappointed with my circumstances, I have a choice: Wallow and stay in the disappointment permanently or find a way to make it matter. After a healthy dose of grieving, I always choose to make it matter. Every time. For the last decade I have used my disappointments to fuel my ability to rise up and help others. I share my experiences. I teach them in coaching groups and private sessions and on in-person and virtual stages. I design programs and books to help people apply the lessons I've learned. Why? Because I hope that someone else will rise up and help others because of the lessons I have shared with them from my own disappointments and setbacks.

Hope is dangerous like that. It comes with the risk of not getting the thing you hoped for, in the way that you hoped it would come. But my friend, I'm here to encourage you today to lean into Hope Deferred when it comes. There is something valuable in it that will equip you to keep going. And that is the real danger of hope!

Hope changes things.

Yes, sometimes hope blows. It knocks the air right out of your lungs and you wonder how you'll ever get back up again. But you will. Hope Deferred is just a place you're passing through — a necessary stop in The Cycle of Dangerous Hope. Lean into it and write it all down. One day when you look back, you'll see it. Hope Deferred will be worked into the ground and your field of hope will be more fertile than it was before.

The when is up to you.

DANGEROUS HOPE

Lean into Hope Deferred when it comes. There is something valuable in it that will equip you to keep going.

SIX
•••
The Cycle of Dangerous Hope in Business

Ask any entrepreneur how they got their start, and I'm willing to bet that their story involves going through The Cycle of Dangerous Hope. They most likely aren't aware of the fact that this is the cycle they went through, so they probably describe it with words like, "I wanted to take what I learned in that experience and help others." Entrepreneurs have an uncanny ability to see the possibilities of Dangerous Hope in the dark valleys of their hardest seasons of life.

Like all the women carrying the torch of entrepreneurship before us, we too have a story that led us to starting our company. Owning a company with your best friend is a challenging endeavor that has a ton of risk behind it. It takes a lot of personal growth and vulnerability to do it effectively. In the seven years that Raychel and I have been in partnership together, we've seen a handful of other women in our community launch businesses together and most of them have since split. Perhaps the reason why we are so committed to building this dream together is because it started nearly three decades ago. In fact, we were barely in junior high.

I met Raychel on a hot summer day at a dusty little Baptist Bible Camp the summer between fifth and sixth grade. We bonded over a love of singing and escaping group activities. Participating in relays that consisted of passing oranges between our knees seemed like the dumbest activity a kid could do in the summer. So, we would hide in our cabin with two other friends while I did my breathing treatments. I would even let Raychel pound my back as part of my treatment to help me cough out the mucus. It was the best excuse ever!

We would gush over cute boys, have deep conversations about faith — well, as deep as fifth graders can get anyway. And we would sing songs and practice our harmony together, dreaming about the future. I was trying to recruit them into my lifelong dream of being a singer and I was absolutely sure we could be the next Point of Grace. They were an all-female contemporary Christian music group comprised of four women who sang beautiful harmonies with meaningful lyrics. I could totally see it in my mind — we would be called the 4-Ever Friends and we would be a hit one day.

Every summer, the four of us would connect again at camp and our band would reunite. But eventually, once we were old enough to start seriously dreaming about the future, we realized that becoming a famous music group wasn't in the cards for us. The band broke up for good and turned into a group of friends that barely kept in touch through the years.

However, Raychel and I continued to grow close. She was the only friend that kept me in her life when she started having kids. Her family was living halfway across the state at the time, and she invited Nate and me to her daughter's baptism. We couldn't make it to that one, but I vowed to make it work when another invitation came in the mail. Our friendship grew close because Raychel was determined to keep me in her life, even though she knew that Nate and I didn't want kids. I was really thankful for that.

On a breezy May afternoon in 2009, Raychel and I found ourselves dreaming about the future again while walking a 5K in the Cystic Fibrosis Foundation Great Strides Walk. We started saying things like, "Wouldn't it be cool if we wrote a book together one day?" And "Oh man, we could share what we've learned in our marriage and our friendship with so many women!" We let those ideas linger in the air like unfinished goals waiting to be assigned a date and time. So our dream of working together wasn't something we just cooked up in 2014 when we started our company. No, it was planted in our hearts when we were just kids. I think that's why it works.

We got the chance to work together in 2013. One of the ways I wanted to make my Dangerous Hope actions matter was by becoming a certified coach so I could help other people make healthy changes in their lives. My first certification was as a Health Coach through the Dr. Sears Wellness Institute. The training I received through that organization equipped me with the skills and curriculum to offer health classes for parents, children, and adults. While I was offering health classes in our area and online, Raychel was busy putting together a lay counseling team at the church we both attended. She had finished her Bachelors in Psychology and Biblical Counseling and was hired on as the counselor at the church. Her vision for the team was to have a group of professionals that could offer a variety of coaching and counseling services for free to the people that needed it but couldn't yet afford it. People in the congregation were familiar with my health coaching classes because I had offered a six-week program as part of the Wednesday night class lineup in January of that year. She admired the health coaching I was doing and asked me to come on board as the official Health Coach. It was a no-brainer.

We had a blast working together, and we discovered that we were much more effective together than as individuals. Raychel had worked to get her life coaching certification along with her counseling degree. I decided to get more certification as well and made a commitment to start classes through Light University to get my official Life Coaching Diploma. During our time together on this counseling team, we also had a radio show. Actually, it started out as my radio show and I called it *The Health Coach Show with Mandy B. Anderson*. However, I hated doing the show alone in the creepy basement studio of the church. So, I invited Raychel to join me. We changed the name to *The Girls on the Big Blue Couch Show* to pay homage to our time of struggle on her big blue couch. We discussed topics on friendship, our experiences of anxiety and depression, how we both encouraged each other to get up off the couch and live our lives again after dark seasons. Basically, it was two besties talking about life, faith, and everything in between and not holding back. It was a big hit. People around the community began referring to us as "The Girls on the Big Blue Couch." And that sparked a new Dangerous Hope dream in our hearts — to embark on the adventure of owning an organization together that would impact the lives of women in our community, and maybe one day, around the world.

It was an amazing feeling to finally be able to make sense of my story in a way that could impact others. Suddenly my Hope Deferred season didn't look like something to regret. Instead, it looked like something that could help inspire others to get back up after life knocked them down.

In January 2014, after a series of events that unraveled the counseling team faster than we could blink, we poured some wine and decided to take control of our dreams and start our own company. We called it Big Blue Couch Coaching, LLC. And we had no idea how many times we were about to embark on The Cycle of Dangerous Hope, or how important the principles of planting would be to the core message of our company. We had no idea that in 2019 we would burn our fields, get rid of some of our core events, and embark on a journey of rebranding that would knock us off course for a few years. None at all.

Our business story this far has gone through The Cycle of Dangerous Hope more times than I can count — at least twice a year, if not once a quarter if I'm honest. If you're thinking about starting a business, or writing a book, or doing anything to plant something meaningful in the soil of your own disappointment, the following pages will be very helpful. That's why I want to take a few moments to inspect our fields with you. There are some things we did right — seeds that we planted intentionally — that need to be celebrated. At the same time, there are so many things we did wrong that fall under the category of weeds. And, although it was challenging, we worked all of the mulch into the ground after we burned our fields. Let's take a few moments to inspect the fields so you can start identifying some of your own seeds, weeds, and mulch in your career or business, too.

PLANTING THE SEEDS OF DANGEROUS HOPE

We've never struggled with planting seeds in our business, actually. That has been the easiest part for us. My point of view has always been to try something out and treat it like a case study —

learn what needs to be learned and tweak it as you go. Some people struggle to start planting seeds and they just keep procrastinating. Not me. I'd rather get to work and start so I know what I'm working with than try to plan it all ahead of time. The seeds we have planted over and over again because of this perspective are:

THE SEEDS OF COURAGE & BOLDNESS: It takes a ton of courage and boldness to branch out on your own and start a company, write a book, or go after your dream as an artist or musician. There will be people that try to "talk sense" into you, and they might be the people closest to you sometimes. They do this because they love you and they don't want you to struggle. However, the seeds of courage and boldness are so important to keep planting because the truth is you *will* struggle! And that's a good thing. The growth is in the struggle. The seeds of courage and boldness will be needed so you have the gumption to get back up again when life knocks you down.

It took courage for my bestie and I to hold on to our dreams and branch out together as a business, walking away from the security of a ministry/non-profit setting. It took boldness for us to stand up for what we believe and put ourselves into the position of owning our company. It took courage and boldness to make a pitch to a television station to be a guest on a morning show — an action that led to a two-year weekly spot on the show, mind you. It took courage and boldness to publish our own books and share our message with the world through a podcast. When you create content of any kind, it means other people will criticize you. The seeds of courage and boldness will help you develop a tough skin. And trust me, it's needed.

THE SEED OF BELIEF: Your belief in yourself and your ability to learn and grow along the way will be necessary to stay the course. There will be circumstances beyond your control — events that don't sell out, launches that flop, friends that turn on you and call you names, extended family members that doubt or downplay your talent, and even internet trolls that tear you down just for the fun of it. Your belief in yourself and your mission is going to have to be rock-solid. Now, that's not to say that you won't have times where it falters. You might. And that's when you sow some extra seeds of belief and look in the mirror and tell yourself to make it matter again. Nobody else will believe in your dreams for you. It's all up to you.

If I hadn't sown the seed of belief, I would have quit right away. Prior to starting our company, I was a job hopper with tons of experience in many industries because I was capable and not afraid of a challenge. Yet I couldn't stay in one place for longer than two years because those jobs never fulfilled me. I believed in this dream of helping people rise up and equipping them with lessons that I had learned long before I signed my name on the LLC paperwork. Every time I felt like giving up along the way, I reminded myself that this was my purpose. I would think back to the moment in the hospital where I looked in the mirror and told myself to make it matter. Just like a dry and thirsty plant that finally drinks in the healing rain after a drought, my belief would perk right back up.

THE SEED OF ACTION: Without this seed, you won't accomplish anything. You will need to take action every day. And let me warn you — many times you won't feel like it! Highlight this next part: Your action should not be dictated by your feelings! Just like your health goals won't magically be reached because you go to the gym one time, your career or business aspirations won't amount to anything without daily planting the seed of action.

I don't know what type of action makes you want to crawl back into bed when you think about taking it, but for me it is the action of an email campaign. The ones where you need to send cold-call emails one-by-one to people you are connected to on LinkedIn but you don't actually know because you suck at connecting with them. Yeah, that's the one. It causes me a ton of stress because it seems like such a daunting task that basically signs you up for daily rejection. But you know what I've learned? This action actually bears much fruit when you do it.

You might think the actions you need to sow are things like creating a business plan, posting the right things on social media, organizing your office, coming up with a daily schedule and sticking to it, creating standard operating procedures in your business so everyone is on the same page, and staying on top of your finances. Those are all necessary actions for sure! But don't neglect the action of email marketing and networking with strangers. That has been the most fruitful action for me lately, and I'm learning to enjoy it! And, if you love networking and that's the easy part for you, go back to the items I listed above and see if there's an action on that list that you dread. Once you find it, you'll know that's the seed of action that you need to plant.

Planting the seeds of Dangerous Hope is something you will never stop doing in life. When you don't know which seeds you are planting and which seeds you are forgetting to plant, you'll keep hitting your head against a wall because you will be planting without a plan. Remember, every farmer needs to map out their fields so they know what they are going to plant and grow. Be intentional with your seed sowing, my friend. It matters.

CONTROLLING THE WEEDS OF FALSE HOPE

There's a teaching in some coaching circles that says if you see a weed popping up in your life, it's growing because you planted it.

Yet, based on the planting principles that my dad taught me, this line of thinking isn't exactly true, is it? Sometimes, weeds just show up in your fields. They might blow in from another field, or they might just be in the soil and you weren't aware. It's pointless to beat yourself up for the weeds because they are just a part of life.

You'd think since I had gone through a season of False Hope in my personal life with my health that I would have easily recognized the signs of it again much sooner in our business. But remember, the weed of False Hope is a perennial weed that grows from the long-established roots of wishful thinking. Just because you pluck them out of one field of hope, like in my personal life, that doesn't mean that you automatically plucked them out of the other field, too. Plucking the weeds out of one field will never automatically cause the weeds in a different field to just disappear. You still have to do the work of weeding — in all the fields. The weed of False Hope was overtaking our field, and it was hiding among other weeds. Here's a few of the biggest ones that hindered our success:

THE WEED OF A POVERTY MINDSET: This can also be called a lack mindset. It's when you believe that there will never be enough or that money will run out. It also happens when you think that money will just flow in and you don't have to be in charge of stewarding it well. When the weed of a poverty mindset is present in business, you will neglect paying attention to your finances. You might be paying bills on time and staying out of a negative balance, but you'll never get to the point of having a bank account that grows beyond the expenses because you won't be aware of what is actually happening in your business.

This was how we operated for the first six years of our partnership. Our company was growing, and we had reached a small level of world-wide impact — one year we shipped books to clients over two different oceans! However, we were not as profitable as it sounds. In fact, we hadn't even cracked six figures yet. In 2018, we reached a financial milestone of bringing in the most revenue we had ever brought in — around $61,000. That's not a bad income for a solo entrepreneur with no overhead and no team. But we were a partnership. Our team was comprised of Raychel and myself, and our two contracted workers. As owners of the company, and the main coaches doing all the work, we had zero dollars to show for our hard work in our personal finances. We were burnt out from working for free and putting everything back into our company.

The weed of a poverty mindset also had me tricked into thinking I could not handle a part-time job while building our business because I had cystic fibrosis. I believed I had a lack of energy and therefore refused to even consider it. This led to my personal finances not growing. Nate and I didn't necessarily take steps backward in our finances, but we definitely weren't getting ahead. I had to pluck out that weed in 2020 and get a part-time job in order to reach our personal goals of owning a home again. Honestly, it has been the best thing for me, both financially and mentally. When you pay attention to the weed of a poverty mindset, you start to see solutions to get rid of it. Paying attention to the finances both in our business and in my home helped get us into a position to kill this weed.

THE WEED OF PRIVILEGE: This one hurts a bit, and I really don't want to admit that it's there. But here's the thing — when we started our company back in 2014, we were two besties with husbands that worked in the oil field and our weed of privilege was that we did not need to make a paycheck for our household. Our families were both in the six-figure club the year we started our company, and because of this we set up the company with all four of us being owners. The husbands were silent owners that invested money into the company, acting as our own line of credit to help cover lean months when just starting out, while Raychel and I did all the work. This meant that we had the privilege of owning a company without the pressure of having to make it profitable. I'll be very candid here; we treated it like a clubhouse in the beginning — like a grown-up version of *The Babysitter's Club*. This led to a rude awakening once the oil bust happened in 2015 and Nate lost his job, while Raychel's husband at the time had a huge drop in his income. Our families could no longer afford to act like an operating loan, and we were forced to find a solution that would make up the difference each month. We did it — by offering more workshop-like events and frequent six-week coaching programs. However, the weed of privilege definitely contributed to our poverty mindset in a way that made it harder for Raychel and I to treat ourselves like we were worth a paycheck.

The weed of privilege is an ugly weed that we don't like to talk about, especially since it shows up in our society so much lately when it comes to the topic of systemic racism in the United States. In fact, that last sentence might make you roll your eyes right now because you might be on the side that doesn't think it exists. However, I challenge you to look at your own life and look at where the weed of privilege might actually be infesting your fields of hope in sneaky ways. Privilege doesn't have to be associated with the color of your skin. It can also be associated with the size of your bank account. If all you've ever known is the world of wealth, then the weed of privilege might be blinding you from the realities of financial struggle. And financial struggles will kill your hope faster than you realized. If you see this weed in your life, in this way, I encourage you to weed it out by pouring some empathy on it and leaning in to learn from the people who have struggled financially. Glean the wisdom they have from going through a situation you maybe haven't been in for a while, or ever. Getting rid of the weed of privilege makes it possible for the seeds of resilience and compassion to grow in your field of hope.

THE WEEDS OF PRIDE & HOLY COWS: The weed of pride is always one that entrepreneurs need to be aware of. Pride will keep you from being teachable and learning from other coaches or experts. It might even keep you from leaning in and listening to your audience so you can offer services or products that they are asking for. However, the weed of pride often grows alongside the weed of holy cows. What's a holy cow? Well, it's like this: In the Old Testament of the Bible there is a story of Moses and the Israelites. Moses went up on the mountain to talk to God and he was gone longer than the Israelites had planned. So, while he was up there, the Israelites asked Moses' brother, Aaron, to make an idol for them so they could start worshipping that idol instead of God. Aaron completely caved into peer pressure and made the people an idol of a golden cow. And then they bowed down and worshipped the idol. When Moses came back down from the mountain, he was furious about what they had done. But the people insisted that the golden cow was holy, and they didn't want to get rid of it.

In business, we can sometimes hold on to holy cow-type idols that hinder our success. When you refuse to get rid of them, you keep yourself from growing. A holy cow can be a logo, a business name that is confusing to others but you love it, or even certain strategies that you refuse to change. For us, it had become the big blue couch itself. For about a year before we rebranded, we refused to look at the fact that maybe part of the problem was our logo and our name. The big blue couch had become a holy cow to us — a symbol of hope and healing that became a crutch somewhere along the way. It's really hard to keep people on a motivated path of growth and rising up when our logo was a literal symbol of rest and laziness! Facing the fact that we had an infection in our field of the weed of holy cows was a hard truth to come to terms with. However, after about a week of processing it, we could see it. And we determined to start weeding with no further hesitation.

WORKING THE MULCH OF HOPE DEFERRED INTO OUR SOIL

We were absolutely weary after we inspected our fields and discovered all of the weeds. Hope seemed frail to us, actually. Our season of working the mulch of Hope Deferred into our soil has not been a fast one. It has actually been a two-year process that started when we rebranded our company and has been prolonged because of the Covid-19 world that we were forced to live in. Our mulch has come in four different forms:

THE MULCH OF MISTAKES: This is the most obvious one. We made mistakes. A lot of them. And we have had to own every single one of them. The beauty in the mulch of mistakes is that the lessons are ripe for the growing. You can't escape making mistakes in life or in business; it is a necessary part of the process. The sooner you accept that, the sooner your hope will recover. You work this mulch into the ground by naming the mistakes and then looking at what you could have done differently and what you learned. Then you map out a new field to grow your seeds of Dangerous Hope again with more wisdom and discernment than before.

THE MULCH OF PERSONAL LIFE ISSUES: Ever feel like you wear a lot of different hats trying to juggle all of your responsibilities? You have a work hat, a friend hat, a home-life hat. I'm here to tell you that this idea of having to wear all the hats, and that none of them will affect each other, is a big fat lie. While you express yourself in different ways in all of those environments, you are still the same person and the circumstances from one "hat" will absolutely affect how you handle circumstances when you put the other "hat" on. There's no way around it. When your personal life is a mess, you will be less effective in your career. Especially if your personal life chaos involves health issues. We had to be willing to let go of the need to achieve and just show up the best we could when personal life issues showed up. Raychel went through a divorce, which meant that the legal ownership of our business was changing since her soon-to-be ex-husband would not be an owner anymore. Both her and I went through miscellaneous health issues, too. Some people quit their businesses when this happens, and other people start businesses because of this happening. Working the mulch of personal life issues into your field will help you implement better self-care practices so you can manage stress better when it comes.

The beauty of working this mulch into our field was that we were able to share the lessons we learned with our clients. It's how we created the foundational content like The Art of the P.A.U.S.E. and Cultivate Honor. It has been the source of most of our teachings, actually. When you work the mulch of personal life issues into your soil, you should see the growth of wisdom, peace, vulnerability, and perspective. The questions I shared in chapter five are how you accomplish this.

THE MULCH OF THE LABEL OF HYPOCRITE: This has been the hardest mulch to work into our fields. When you teach content about personal growth and conflict resolution, you paint a target on your back. People put you on a pedestal and expect you to be perfect, never making mistakes. And then if you do make a mistake, and inadvertently hurt someone in the process, they can sometimes get mean. This has happened to me and it hurts.

I don't pretend to have it all figured out, or to even live out all of the things I teach with perfect precision. Not at all. In fact, I'm pretty vulnerable about my shortcomings. I've had people take that vulnerability and throw it back in my face by calling me a hypocrite. And it hurts. I believe that our words matter, and I don't throw labels around because I value people. I understand that we all have days where we think things that aren't true, or don't actually portray how we feel about a person on a good day. We all have permission to feel our feelings, but we should be able to process them without tearing someone down.

Someone close to me once sent me an angry letter — by certified mail, mind you — and called me a hypocrite in it. This person had every right to feel her feelings about the circumstances that surrounded the situation, and I knew she would be feeling these types of things. That's why I gave her space to process and heal. However, I was also dealing with feelings about the situation that went far beyond just her involvement in it. I wasn't ready to talk about things at the moment she insisted we should, and because I upheld a boundary of "not yet," she took that as a door slam of "not ever." In her anger, she wrote every mean thing she could think of and made sure I got it. That resulted in deep hurt, and a questioning of my character that affected how I showed up in my company. I got quiet and stopped writing. I started to believe that maybe I really was a hypocrite, and maybe I shouldn't share anything with people because maybe all I actually did was hurt them. It has taken me a few years to work the mulch of this label of hypocrite into the ground. I had to walk through the very content I shared in chapter five to gain perspective, and I've had many sessions with my counselor to help process the hurt. In doing so, my counselor gave me wise advice that has helped me work this mulch into the ground, so I was ready to plant the seeds of hope again. "Never let someone else's hurt and lack of character stop you from sharing what you know in your heart you were born to share." That's what she told me. And it was exactly the thing I needed to hear to be able to make it matter again.

Working the mulch of the label of hypocrite requires you to face the truth that as you grow, there might be moments where you do act like a hypocrite. However, if you are a person that cares about your character, then acting like a hypocrite in a tough moment does not mean you are one at your core. I'm here to tell you that you are allowed to make mistakes. You are allowed to change your mind. When these things happen, lean into the vulnerability of it and be willing to apologize when needed and explain why the new point of view has arrived. And remember this truth: How you handle a circumstance is on you; how other people handle you handling that circumstance is on them.

∙∙∙

In the Fall of 2020, Raychel and I found ourselves on a much-needed business retreat road trip. While trying to find the charming little Bible camp that we would be staying at, we wound up lost on a dusty dirt road in the middle of Minnesota. The GPS on my phone decided to take us on a scenic route. A canopy of golden trees created a gorgeous tunnel to drive through, and in that moment, we had an epiphany: We actually hated making online courses! So much! That was not our jam. We missed the process of creating physical books that women devoured. We missed the feeling of creating events with in-person and virtual audiences. Someone once told us that you should define your niche, not so that you never work with people outside of it, but so that you are clear on who you will be working with the most. That advice helped us realize it was time to reclaim our fields and return to our original why: To help women rise up, lead well, and live with intention. We were done trying to be palatable to the people that would never actually put their money where their mouth was to work with us, yet gave us all the opinions of what they thought we should be doing. We wanted to teach leadership skills to a group of women that are usually overlooked in the leadership world — the women just starting out, stuck in the messy middle, not yet making the big paychecks, or clueless to the reality that they are in fact leaders even if they don't have a fancy title.

My husband had been ready to relinquish his ownership in the company for quite some time, but I had been afraid to take the reins without his input. Now I was ready. Both Raychel and I were. We decided to start the process of officially dissolving Big Blue Couch Coaching, LLC and the RAYMA Team DBA that we had set up under it, and we bravely filled out the paperwork to make RAYMA Team, LLC a 100% women-owned company.

We had become the women we always knew we could be, and we were ready to make decisions about our company that weren't influenced by anyone else. We were RAYMA Team — the women that were resilient, authentic, said yes to the right opportunities, motivated ourselves, and assertively took action and trusted our instincts. We were ready to rise up in this new era and reclaim our land.

•••

When you can finally admit your mistakes and rise up because of them, you know that you're ready to lead the way for others. Some leaders are leaders in name only because they are at the top of the chain at their company or in their department. But the leaders of Dangerous Hope become leaders worth following when they go through The Cycle of Dangerous Hope again and again on purpose.

And, just in case you feel like this chapter doesn't really apply to you, I want to reassure you that you can be a leader of Dangerous Hope even if you don't identify as an entrepreneur. In fact, I've come up with a new name for this type of leader. As we turn the page to the final chapter, you'll discover how you can step into this new title.

When you can finally admit your mistakes and rise up because of them, you know that you're ready to lead.

SEVEN
•••
Becoming an Agent of Dangerous Hope

In the farming world, a crop adjuster is the person that inspects your field when you file an insurance claim. They are a representative, an agent if you will, of the insurance company. In The Cycle of Dangerous Hope, the crop adjusters have an official title: Agents of Dangerous Hope. It sounds so official, and a bit like something you would find in the Marvel Comics Universe. I imagine them standing tall and stoic like Agent Coulson in *Avengers*.

When it comes to sharing hope with the world, we all have the ability to be an Agent of Dangerous Hope. Once we understand the process of The Cycle of Dangerous Hope, and we inspect the fields of our own lives both personally and professionally, we can be an advocate that inspires others in meaningful ways.

The Agents of Dangerous Hope that have impacted my life the most are the advocates and heroes of hope that have stayed committed to their mission no matter how many times they got knocked down — no matter who is for or against them.

One such person is a woman named Doris Tulcin. I have never met Doris. In fact, up until a year ago I didn't even know she existed. However, her life has significantly impacted mine, as well as the entire community of cystic fibrosis patients around the world.

The year was 1955. Doris was the mother of a two-year-old daughter named Annie. Annie had CF and was given one year to live. Determined to save the life of her child, Doris did what moms do. She found other parents who also had kids with CF and together they formed a support group that would later become known as the Cystic Fibrosis Foundation.

Now, they didn't have the answers to their children's health problems. But what they did have was a Dangerous Hope that they could make a difference in a big way. Their strategy for doing this was to raise awareness of this disease and raise money that could go toward research to one day find a cure. Doris was well-connected, thanks to her father's work in the oil industry. She had grown up in the world of philanthropy and was used to fundraisers with wealthy people. Doris diligently learned from the leaders of successful organizations to understand what needed to be done to turn this hope into a reality, and it paid off. Here's the highlight reel of what they accomplished at the Cystic Fibrosis Foundation over the course of 65 years:

- In 1961 they developed care centers focused on the disease. Because of the diverse nature of this disease, medical professionals had no standard of care to follow for it. These care centers changed that. Doctors and families now had a community of people to lean on for support and a standard protocol for care that helped improve the quality of life for patients that had previously died before they reached adolescence.

- In 1982 they gathered top-notch scientists to establish a research development program to improve their understanding of CF. The seeds of hope they had planted over twenty years prior were finally coming to fruition. This research development program led to the discovery of the CF gene in 1989. (It also sparked the Human Genome Project, which was a giant breakthrough in our ability as humans to understand human genetics. Look it up because the internet can explain it way better than I can. All I know is that it's a big deal, and it happened because of the research that began with cystic fibrosis.)

- The research that the Cystic Fibrosis Foundation helped fund in the 1990's allowed them to develop new medications that extended the quality and the length of life for CF patients. One of those drugs was a daily medication called Pulmozyme® that patients take once a day to help thin the thick mucus in the lungs. Another drug was an antibiotic called TOBI®. It was "the first aerosolized antibiotic designed for CF, which is proven to reduce hospital stays and improve lung functions." Personally, I have been on Pulmozyme since it was approved and I take TOBI often when I'm in the hospital for a tune-up or have a pesky lung infection (like *Pseudomonas aeruginosa*) that doesn't go away.

- From 2010—2012, when I was going through my own Cycle of Dangerous Hope and not doing my medicine, the CFF was busy creating the first drug to treat the underlying cause of this disease. They called it Kalydeco®, and it became the first drug that moved the needle closer to a cure. However, it only helped up to 60% of the CF population. So, they kept working.

- By October 2019, a drug called Trikafta™ was fast tracked to the marketplace. It is the first triple-combination therapy for people with CF and it is a game-changer. It currently helps up to 90% of the CF population. Patients went off lung transplant lists once they started taking this medication because their lung functions improved so drastically.

I started taking Trikafta in February 2020. Within an hour of taking the first dose, my lungs felt different. I started coughing up gunk that had been in my lungs for who knows how long. My ability to sing like I had in high school returned. And, my body started absorbing nutrients normally for the first time ever! No longer was I the skinny chick with chicken legs and a bony butt. I was a woman with junk in her trunk and strong legs who never coughed and had more energy than she had in years! My lung functions improved from 72% to 82% on this drug and I'm still holding out hope that they can keep getting higher.

When I tell this story, I get choked up because I can't imagine where any of us CFers would be had Doris not been the Agent of Dangerous Hope that she was. She is. Her Dangerous Hope impacted the CF community in the 50s, the 60s, the 70s… and decades later it has impacted me. I'm alive today because she activated Dangerous Hope.

Just think about how many times she must have gone through The Cycle of Dangerous Hope.

She planted seeds of hope every time she put together a fundraiser. Every time she connected new families with the CFF office in their state, more seeds of hope were planted. Every time the

CFF reached a new milestone, hope grew and more seeds were planted while others were sprouting up.

She definitely became a pro at controlling the weeds of False Hope when the politics of raising money and distributing that money tried to distract others from the goal of providing funding for the only thing that would one day provide a cure: Research. Maybe there were moments where the weeds of False Hope tried to trick others into just being thankful for the progress that was already made and stop fighting so hard. But there was Doris, cutting those weeds down to protect her seeds of Dangerous Hope.

She had to have worked the mulch of Hope Deferred into her field of hope again and again when news of CF patients dying reached her desk in the decades where the research team hadn't even been developed yet. Or in the moments where a door was closed in a meeting about more funding. Maybe there were times of Hope Deferred in the moments when Annie had an infection.

She must have gone through all of these moments because she's human. But again and again she kept fighting. Planting. Weeding. Mulching. And because she didn't give up, the patients and families affected by this disease — as well as the scientists and medical professionals who have worked diligently to find a cure — all had their lives changed for the better.

And Annie? Well, in 2020 Annie celebrated her 67th birthday.

That is the power of Dangerous Hope, and an example of what happens when one person dedicates their life to a cause bigger than herself.

∙∙∙

I'm willing to bet there are some Agents of Dangerous Hope that have impacted your life as well. People you probably have never met that gave you hope in big ways simply because of their story and the example of hope that they lived out. Here's a few more of mine:

JESUS CHRIST

The OG of Dangerous Hope is none other than Jesus Christ. Whether we share the same faith or not, it's pretty evident that the Dangerous Hope he sparked has lasted for thousands of years, even past his death.

When you grow up in church hearing about Jesus's life, you can grow numb to the power and even the hope of him. It becomes a story that you know by rote, but not always by heart.

There is no denying that Jesus Christ sparked such a Dangerous Hope of eternal life beyond earth that he not only died for it, he inspired others to take up their cross and follow in his footsteps. Whether you believe the Gospel or not, there's no bigger Agent of Dangerous Hope than that! And, if you want to meet him, all you have to do is crack open the pages of a Bible. You'll find his life story in the books of Matthew, Mark, Luke, and John.

ZACH SOBIECH

One of the stories that really impacted me several years ago is that of a young man named Zachary Sobiech. I read about his life back in 2014 in the book, *Fly A Little Higher,* written by his mom, Laura Sobiech.

Zach battled a rare form of cancer called osteosarcoma. He was also an aspiring musician and in 2012 he wrote a song called, Clouds. It was a hit. His song has inspired millions of people. He passed away in 2013 when he was only 18 years old. He didn't get to fully experience the life he hoped for. He didn't get to hear raving fans at his concerts or have a long career as a songwriter. Oh, he tasted small glimpses of it during his life on earth. However, the seeds of Dangerous Hope that he planted during his lifetime extended years beyond his death.

In 2020 his life story became a movie aptly called, *Clouds*. Adapted from the book his mom wrote, this movie shared his life story in ways that brought more hope to people during a pandemic than he could ever have imagined when he walked the earth.

Before he died, Zach recognized that he had an opportunity to share hope with people even after his life on earth was finished. He started the Zachary Sobiech Osteosarcoma Fund to help raise money to find a cure for this rare form of cancer. His royalty fees from his music are still raising money to find a cure to this day. Zach is proof that it is possible to turn your disappointments into something meaningful. He is a shining example of an Agent of

Dangerous Hope who made sure to make his life matter long after he is gone.

DOROTHY ANDERSEN

I recently learned about this woman in a book called *Breath from Salt*, by Bijal P. Trivedi. She tells the fascinating history of the discovery of cystic fibrosis and the history of the CF Foundation. I highly recommend it!

In the book, I discovered that Dorothy Andersen was an M.D. in the 1930s who noticed that cystic fibrosis was not celiac disease like doctors had thought it was back then. They say she was a rare woman for her time. An only child, she was born in North Carolina and an orphan by the age of nineteen. She dedicated her life to her work. One day while performing an autopsy on a three-year-old child said to have died of celiac disease, she noticed that the lungs were heavy and filled with thick mucus. She also noticed that the pancreas of this child looked nothing like the pancreas of celiac disease. Dorothy scoured medical journals from across the world to find other cases that resembled the ones she was seeing in her practice. Her dedication to learning about this mysterious disease led to significant discoveries in the late 30s and 40s.

She was known for keeping in touch with the parents of her CF patients and even sent them letters with recipes to help the CF kids gain weight. There's no doubt in my mind that without her hope of finding answers, many parents would not have had the extended years of life that they had with their sick children. Her hope mattered.

MY PRE-SALE INVESTORS

In October 2020, a group of hopeful readers believed in this message enough to pre-order copies of this very book without knowing when it would get into their hands. I had started to believe that I had nothing valuable to offer anymore. Somewhere in the midst of rebranding our company and trying to stay afloat during a pandemic, my hope ran dry. I began to question everything I wanted to share with the world.

And then I got an opportunity to embark on the journey of a pre-sale campaign to get this book in front of publishers. To my surprise, I pre-sold 139 copies. Readers were messaging me about their excitement and belief in this project and it was the boost of hope I needed to rise up and do it.

If you are one of the precious souls that pre-ordered this book during this campaign, I want you to know that to me, you are an Agent of Dangerous Hope. You planted a seed of hope in me again that my message could impact others. I've held onto that more than you could ever know during this process of writing the book and finding the right publisher for it. Don't ever think that your simple actions don't matter. To authors, every time you buy a book, share a book, and send a message to us about our books, you become

Agents of Dangerous Hope to us. You give us hope that our words matter to you.

YOU

And finally, one of the Agents of Dangerous Hope that inspires me is You. Yes, you, the precious soul reading this very book. You inspire me because you cared enough about keeping your hope alive that you picked up this book and actually read it. You are a teachable person who cares so much about turning your disappointments into something meaningful.

As we end our time together, I want you to think about your life and where you are at in The Cycle of Dangerous Hope:

> Have you planted the seeds of Dangerous Hope already? If so, remember to also sow the characteristics needed to handle and maintain what you are hoping for. Sow the seeds of action, belief, boldness, courage, faith, assertiveness, and risk-taking. Don't just throw your seeds of Dangerous Hope blindly into the wind. Be intentional about it. Map out your fields and clearly define how you will plant something meaningful in the soil of your disappointments.

> Are you prepared for the setbacks and ready to control the weed of False Hope even if it means burning a field to start over and rebuild? You better be. Don't get caught up in toxic

positivity, thinking that nothing bad will happen as long as you just believe. You're smarter than that now. Be prepared. Confront the weeds of denial, fear, avoidance, pride, lying, manipulation, and irresponsibility. Cut out the weeds of a poverty mindset, privilege, and holy cows. What you are hoping for, matters. Handle it with the care and respect that it deserves because the people you will help on the other side are worth it.

Or are you in the process of working the mulch of Hope Deferred into the ground so you can turn that disappointment into something meaningful again? If so, don't give up when you get weary. When the lies creep in trying to convince you that it doesn't matter so why hope anymore, cut them down. Work in the mulch of restoration, remaining faith, and understanding something better. Take the mulch of mistakes, personal life issues, and the label of hypocrite and grow something so meaningful from them that others can't help but want to follow your lead because of your example.

Wherever you are at in the cycle, I want to remind you to stick with it. Don't be afraid to wrestle with hope. To plant it. To control the weeds. To work that mulch into your ground so it stays fertile. It all matters, my friend. And there's no shame in burning your fields to start over with new purpose.

•••

Several months ago, I was having another deep conversation with my dad. We were talking about a complicated situation with some people that we know. Decisions had to be made about the wellbeing of someone that was struggling with an illness and instead of making some hard choices, the people that were in charge of making those decisions were doing nothing. Well, not nothing. They were praying, which is important, especially if you are a person of faith. However, they were ignoring the obvious signs that medical intervention was a necessary partner to their prayers. It was a very difficult situation.

We were sitting on the pontoon that was docked in the sand in the backyard of our new condo. It was a beautiful sunny, summer day in North Dakota with the water from the river sparkling in the background. Shaded by the canopy, my dad laid his head back on the cushion of the seat and said, "Mandy, hope is not a strategy."

His words have been on repeat in my mind ever since.

"Hope is not a strategy."

Have you heard this saying, too? I'm willing to bet my grande Starbucks Caramel Macchiato (with coconut milk, thank you) that you have. In fact, it's so popular that if you Google it, you'll find 1,010,000,000 results! If that's not proof that people are really wrestling with hope, then I don't know what is!

But what if Dangerous Hope *became* the strategy we started using? What if we started to lean into The Cycle of Dangerous Hope so we could master it? What would happen?

I think we would all rise up as Agents of Dangerous Hope if we did. We would plant the seeds of wisdom, resilience, discernment, courage, strength, and more hope than we could harvest. We would learn from our mistakes, anticipate the setbacks, and keep taking calculated action. We would get so good at controlling the weeds of False Hope and working the mulch of Hope Deferred into our fields that our harvest time would speed up because we would waste less time in fear, worry, and doubt. If Dangerous Hope became our strategy, our hope would not only be effective, it would be dangerous to the mediocrity and hopelessness that used to taunt us.

So, promise me one thing before we go. Promise me that you'll embrace Dangerous Hope as your strategy from this point forward. Never stop hoping. The moment you stop hoping is the moment that you risk never becoming the person you could be to help the people you could impact. When it seems like hope is lost, remember the principles that you learned in this book. Remember the pep talk I told myself when I looked in the mirror that night in the hospital. No matter what your new normal looks like, work the mulch into the ground so you can plant new seeds of Dangerous Hope and turn those disappointments into something meaningful again and again.

Dangerous Hope will be the only thing stronger than your fear. Make it matter.

DANGEROUS HOPE

DANGEROUS HOPE WILL BE THE ONLY THING STRONGER THAN YOUR FEAR. MAKE IT MATTER.

ACKNOWLEDGEMENTS

•••

I am forever grateful for the precious souls that have helped this book become a reality.

NATE ANDERSON

The first person I want to thank for going on this journey of Dangerous Hope with me is my husband, Nate. Handsome, thank you for being my number one cheerleader. Your constant support and encouragement means the world to me. I love you so much.

RAYCHEL PERMAN

You are the best friend a girl could ask for, and a fabulous CEO. Thank you for always taking the time to listen to my ideas, read my words, and help me hash out the content for this book. And thank you for always believing in me, even when I was lost in Hope Deferred. I love you. Real. Always. Okay.

MY PARENTS

I love you both so much. Thank you for being the wonderful parents that you are, and for allowing me to share the hardest parts of our story so that others can be encouraged. I hope our story makes you proud.

DR. LANCE PRESSER

Thank you for the valuable feedback you've given me over the last two years as I worked on this message. The questions you had, and the details you wanted to know about what it felt like to be so sick with CF, helped me write a better book. I hope as you read it, you'll think to yourself, "It's not terrible."

RACHAEL NEVA, PHOTOGRAPHER

Your idea to pour my pills into the sand for the cover photo was brilliant. The photos you edited are gorgeous and it was a blast to work with you. Thank you for helping me create such a powerful vision for this book. Your art matters.

JACLYN REUTER, EDITOR

Thank you for your encouragement and guidance through this process. You helped me dig deep and become a better writer. I am so thankful that we connected in the Ladyboss Fargo-Moorhead Facebook Group.

LEE CONSTANTINE AND THE PUBLISHIZER TEAM

I am certain that this book would not be a reality right now had it not been for you reaching out to me through LinkedIn back in February of 2020. Thank you for encouraging me to take a leap of faith with this book. The pre-order campaign we did in October 2020 was the boost of hope that I needed to start writing again. And the valuable feedback you and your team gave me after reading the first three chapters helped me craft this message into one that had focus and heart. I'm so very thankful that you believed in this message the way that you did.

LOREN NIEUWSMA, MY SPEAKER COACH FOR TEDX BISMARCK

Thank you for being blunt and helping me craft a solid TEDx Talk. Technically, the TEDx Talk was done a year before this book was completed, and the outline we came up with helped me find focus in this book. Thank you for challenging me to find a compelling way to tell this story in a way that matters to the audience. In my opinion, you're the best Speaker Coach ever. Anyone would be lucky to work with you.

CORPORATE SPONSORS

A very special thank you to Dakota Home Care and DTN Staffing for sponsoring this book before it was ever written. Meeting with your leadership team this past year has been a wonderful experience. I am honored to have your support. DHC and DTN are the cream of the crop.

JEHOVAH RAPHA

Thank you for restoring my health and giving me a second chance at life. I hope when I meet you face-to-face at the gates of Heaven, you say, "Well done."

NOTES

CHAPTER 2

Page 26
- And now she's a billionaire: https://harrypotter.bloomsbury.com/uk/jk-rowling-biography/
- Let's look at a few other inspiring, famous examples: https://small-bizsense.com/10-famous-entrepreneurs-who-failed-in-business-before-becoming-successful/

Page 32
- She shares her journey, and her passion, in a heartfelt episode entitled, "Your Goals Don't Give a Crap About How You Feel": https://podcasts.apple.com/us/podcast/13-your-goals-dont-give-crap-about-how-you-feel-april/id1456804468?i=1000441026238

Page 33
- And Kim had hope: https://podcasts.apple.com/us/podcast/57-the--dmn-plan-with-kim-nagle/id1456804468?i=1000491539381

Page 44
- The University of Massachusetts Amherst describes weeds like this: https://ag.umass.edu/turf/fact-sheets/guide-to-weed-life-cycles
- Another source mentioned: http://www.american-lawns.com/problems/weeds/annual-vs-perennial.html

CHAPTER 3

Page 52
- Inspection at the time of sowing: http://www.bafra.gov.bt/wp-content/uploads/2015/06/Guidelines-for-Field-and-Seed-Inspection.pdf

Page 59
- According to Medlineplus.gov: https://medlineplus.gov/genetics/understanding/consult/treatment/

Page 63
- Truly listen — not to defend, but to understand: https://podcasts.apple.com/us/podcast/59-becoming-aware-with-content-creator-bobby-foster/id1456804468?i=1000493192922

CHAPTER 4

Page 87
- And the woman stands firm in her belief and simply says, "no.": Jason Selvig, Twitter post, January 21, 2021: "It was honor to talk to a Trump supporter the exact moment Joe Biden was sworn in": https://twitter.com/jasonselvig/status/1352374957330862082

Page 93
- According to an info graph that they posted on November 14th, 2020 our daily totals looked like this: North Dakota Department of Health Facebook post, November 14, 2020: https://www.facebook.com/ndhealth/photos/10159062933232445
- Take a look at the numbers that the North Dakota Department of Health posted on February 4, 2021: North Dakota Department of Health Facebook post, February 4, 2021: https://www.facebook.com/ndhealth/photos/10159289072642445

Page 95
- "In psychiatry there is a certain condition known as…": Viktor E. Frankl, *Man's Search for Meaning* (Boston: Beacon Press, 2006), p. 10
- "Many times, hopes for a speedy end to the war…": Viktor E. Frankl, *Man's Search for Meaning* (Boston: Beacon Press, 2006), p. 34

Page 96
- "The phrase "toxic positivity" refers to…" K. Lukin Ph.D., "Toxic Positivity: Don't Always Look on the Bright Side," *Psychology Today,* August 1, 2019, https://www.psychologytoday.com/us/blog/the-man-cave/201908/toxic-positivity-dont-always-look-the-bright-side

Page 97
- The circumstances created by the spread of Covid-19…": S. Singh, "Workplace Stress and Anxiety After Covid-19," *Business.com,* September 11, 2020, https://www.business.com/articles/workplace-stress-anxiety-covid-19/

CHAPTER 5

Page 121
- "One of the great mistakes...": David W. Swanson, Twitter post, May 21, 2021: https://twitter.com/davidswanson/status/1395825400765370371

Page 125
- According to an article published by the CDC on August 14, 2020: https://www.cdc.gov/mmwr/volumes/69/wr/mm6932a1.htm
- Another source, published on June 4, 2020, stated that "48% of Americans are feeling down, depressed, or hopeless during the Covid-19 pandemic.": https://usafacts.org/articles/45-americans-are-feeling-down-depressed-or-hopeless-during-covid-19-pandemic/

CHAPTER 6

Page 152
- The Art of the P.A.U.S.E. and Cultivate Honor resources are available at https://www.raymateam.com/store

CHAPTER 7

Page 161
- Here's the highlight reel of what they accomplished at the Cystic Fibrosis Foundation over the course of 65 years: https://www.cff.org/Research/About-Our-Research/Research-Milestones/

ABOUT THE AUTHOR

•••

Mandy B. Anderson is a Keynote Speaker, Author, and the Co-Founder of RAYMA Team, LLC. She equips women with the skills they need to rise up, lead well, and live with intention. Anderson vulnerably shares her story of living with cystic fibrosis, and overcoming deep losses and mistakes in life, to encourage others to courageously live their lives to the fullest no matter what they face.

Mandy is a Certified Life Coach, a Certified L.E.A.N. Health Coach, Co-Host of the She Who Overcomes™ Podcast, and was awarded the honor of being in the Top 25 Women in Business for 2020 by Prairie Business Magazine. She lives by the water in North Dakota with her husband, Nate, and their fur baby, Indigo, where she sips her coffee every morning and watches the sunrise. Connect with her at www.mandybanderson.com.

Made in the USA
Monee, IL
20 July 2021